Chris Higgins

Travel better, enjoy more

ULYSSES
Travel Guides

Offices

U.S.A.: Ulysses Travel Guides, 305 Madison Avenue, Suite 1166, New York, NY 10165, ☎ 1-877-542-7247, info@ulysses.ca, www.ulyssesguides.com

CANADA: Ulysses Travel Guides, 4176 Saint-Denis, Montréal, Québec, H2W 2M5, ☎ (514) 843-9447 or 1-877-542-7247, ✆(514) 843-9448, info@ulysses.ca, www.ulyssesguides.com

EUROPE Les Guides de Voyage Ulysse SARL, BP 159, 75523 Paris Cedex 11, France, ☎ 01 43 38 89 50, ✆01 43 38 89 52, voyage@ulysse.ca, www.ulyssesguides.com

Distributors

U.S.A.: The Globe Pequot Press, 246 Goose Lane, Guilford, CT 06437 - 0480, ☎1-800-243-0495, Fax: 800-820-2329, sales@globe-pequot.com

CANADA: Ulysses Books & Maps, 4176 Saint-Denis, Montréal, Québec, H2W 2M5, ☎ (514) 843-9882, ext.2232, 800-748-9171, Fax: 514-843-9448, info@ulysses.ca, www.ulyssesguides.com

GREAT BRITAIN AND IRELAND: World Leisure Marketing, Unit 11, Newmarket Court, Newmarket Drive, Derby DE24 8NW, ☎ 1 332 57 37 37, Fax: 1 332 57 33 99, office@wlmsales.co.uk

SCANDINAVIA: Scanvik, Esplanaden 8B, 1263 Copenhagen K, DK, ☎ (45) 33.12.77.66, Fax: (45) 33.91.28.82

SPAIN: Altaïr, Balmes 69, E-08007 Barcelona, ☎ 454 29 66, Fax: 451 25 59, altair@globalcom.es

SWITZERLAND: OLF, P.O. Box 1061, CH-1701 Fribourg, ☎ (026) 467.51.11, Fax: (026) 467.54.66

OTHER COUNTRIES: Contact Ulysses Books & Maps, 4176 Saint-Denis, Montréal, Québec, H2W 2M5, ☎ (514) 843-9882, ext.2232, ☎ 800-748-9171, Fax: 514-843-9448, info@ulysses.ca, www.ulyssesguides.com

Cataloguing-in-Publication Data (see p 6)
© October 2001, Ulysses Travel Guides.
All rights reserved. Printed in Canada
ISBN 2-89464-396-9

I come from a place that likes grandeur
it likes large gestures
it is not inhibited by flourish
it is a rhetorical society
it is a society of physical performance
it is a society of style

Derek Walcott
Lucian poet and playwright

Table of Contents

Write to Us

The information contained in this guide was correct at press time. However, mistakes can slip in, omissions are always possible, places can disappear, etc. The authors and publisher hereby disclaim any liability for loss or damage resulting from omissions or errors.

We value your comments, corrections and suggestions, as they allow us to keep each guide up to date. The best contributions will be rewarded with a free book from Ulysses Travel Guides. All you have to do is write us at the following address and indicate which title you would be interested in receiving (see the list at the end of the guide).

Ulysses Travel Guides

305 Madison Avenue
Suite 1166, New York
NY 10165

4176 St. Denis Street
Montréal, Québec
Canada H2W 2M5

www.ulyssesguides.com

Author	*Editing Assistance*	**Artistic Director**
Chris Higgins	Raphaël Corbeil	Patrick Farei (Atoll)
Editor	**Page Layout**	**Illustrations**
Jacqueline Grekin	Raphaël Corbeil	Émilie Desmarais
		Vincent Desruisseaux
Publisher	**Cartographer**	
Pascale Couture	Patrick Thivierge	**Photography**
		Cover page
Copy Editing	**Computer Graphics**	Chris Higgins
Eileen Connolly	André Duchesne	*Inside pages*
		Chris Higgins

Thanks

Chris Higgins: my parents, Margaret and Michael Higgins; Dafna Avisar; Innocent and the Calixte family; Jacqueline Grekin; Robert Devaux; Patrick Thivierge; and the staff at the St. Lucia Tourist Board in Castries and Soufrière, particularly Maria Hunt and Maria Fowell at the head office in Castries.

Ulysses Travel Guides: We acknowledge the financial support of the Government of Canada through the Book Publishing Industry Development Program (BPIDP) for our publishing activities. We would also like to thank the Québec government – SODEC income tax program for book publication.

Cataloguing-in-Publication Data

Higgins, Chris

    St. Lucia

    (Ulysses Travel Guides)
    Includes index.

    ISBN 2-89464-396-9

    1. Saint Lucia - Guidebook. I. Title. III. Series.

| F2100.H53 2001 | 917.2984304 | C2001-940631-2 |

List of Maps

Map Symbols

❶	Tourist information	◓	Park
✈	Airport	⊘	Beach
🚌	Bus station	▲	Mountain
☀	Lighthouse	⸸	Church
✉	Post office		

Symbols

≡	Air conditioning
all incl.	All inclusive
bkfst incl.	Breakfast included
⊗	Fan
⇌	Fax number
⊘	Fitness centre
fb	Full board (lodging + 3 meals)
½ b	Half board (lodging + 2 meals)
K	Kitchenette
pb	Private bathroom
≈	Pool
ℜ	Restaurant
ℝ	Refrigerator
▣	Safe
sb	Shared bathroom
☎	Telephone number
⊛	Whirlpool
🦪	Ulysses's favourite

ATTRACTION CLASSIFICATION

★	Interesting
★★	Worth a visit
★★★	Not to be missed

HOTEL CLASSIFICATION

Unless otherwise indicated, the prices in the guide are
for one standard room, double occupancy in high season.

RESTAURANT CLASSIFICATION

$	$10 or less
$$	$10 to $20
$$$	$20 to $30
$$$$	$30 or more

The prices in the guide are for a meal for one
person, not including drinks and tip.

All prices in this guide are in EC dollars.

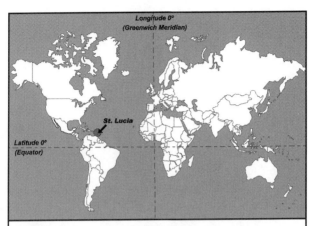

Where is St. Lucia?

©ULYSSES

ST. LUCIA	
Capital:	Castries
Language:	English
Population:	156,000 inhab.
Area:	616 km

St. Martin
St. Barts
**St. Kitts
and Nevis**
Antigua
Montserrat
Guadeloupe
Marie-Galante
Dominica
Martinique
ST. LUCIA
Barbados
St. Vincent
Grenadines
Grenada

*Atlantic
Ocean*

**Dominican
Republic**
**Puerto
Rico**
*Caribbean
Sea*

Venezuela
Colombia
Guyana

*Atlantic
Ocean*

Portrait

From exotic windswept savannah coastlines to mountains and lush rain forests, St. Lucia offers travellers much more than just white sandy beaches.

Beneath the peaks of the magnificent Pitons, there are coral reefs and marine parks, nature reserves, therapeutic spring baths, waterfalls and dozens of secluded coves. In the midst of this natural diversity and beauty is a growing ecotourism industry, one of the most exciting developments on the island. Where the main attraction here was once just sand and surf, visitors to St. Lucia now have many other ways of experiencing this island's beauty, such as scuba diving, hiking, whale-watching, camping, horseback riding or even mountain biking.

St. Lucia's captivating landscape may well lure visitors initially, but it's the people who keep them coming back. Even among West Indians, Lucians are known for their warmth and courtesy. The smooth, wrinkle-free skin of many Lucian faces is perhaps why they come across as genuinely relaxed and easygoing. They possess the friendly, proud spirit of people from a bountiful nation. St. Lucia also has a thriving Creole culture and the sounds of patois can still be heard in many regions of the island. Many restaurants feature Creole cuisine with local dishes such as lambi or conch and callaloo soup. Festivals, like the extremely popular *Jounen Kwéyòl*, have communities across the island celebrating their cultural roots with traditional music, dance, food and costumes.

To get the most out of your trip to St. Lucia, explore as much of the island as you can. On an island where you can drive from one end to the other in half a day, most attractions are within reach wherever you stay. The selection of detailed maps in this guidebook will make it easier for you to journey off the main roads on your own. If possible, stay at several hotels, preferably in different regions of the island. The accommodation listings cover the whole island and include a broad range of styles and budgets, from deluxe resorts to charming and affordable guesthouses.

One last word about Lucian hospitality. The first time I arrived in St. Lucia at Vigie Airport, an anxious feeling set in. It was the kind of feeling travellers get when they arrive late in a strange place. I ambled down the long driveway with my backpack, terribly overdressed and overheated, and stuffed myself into a minibus bound for Castries. At the end of the ride, I asked a man next to me how to get to Soufrière. Gently, he grabbed my arm, led me down two blocks, through the market and across a busy street to a line of vans. Pointing at the coveted passenger seat, he spoke a few quick words in patois to the driver, and then turned to me and said "this man will make sure you get to a hotel in Soufrière." I took my seat and watched as my guide dodged the traffic and thought, "I must be in the right place."

Geography

From a distance, St. Lucia is a silhouette of steep curves and broad lines. Moving

Volcanoes and Land Formation in the Caribbean

The earth's crust is divided up like a huge jigsaw puzzle. The place where these pieces meet is called a fault plane. The entire chain of Caribbean islands lies above a fault zone. When plates collide into one another, an enormous amount of friction is created, heating up the surrounding layers of sedimentary rock and turning it into lava, or molten magma. As the pressure builds, this lava rises and is released through holes in the earth's surface or volcanoes. After the lava cools, it hardens into igneous rock, forming a series of ridges that radiate out from the cone of the volcano, like spokes on a bicycle wheel. In this way, an island is born. The valleys between these ridges channel successive layers of magma into new ridge systems and expand the island's landmass until the eruptions cease.

closer, the tiny coves, lush green leaves and jagged edges of the landscape come into view. It soon becomes apparent that there are many ways of seeing this island.

St. Lucia sits at the heart of the Lesser Antilles, the Caribbean region extending east of Puerto Rico to the northern coast of Venezuela. It is one of a thin line of islands known as the Windwards that cuts across the rough Atlantic to form the tail end of the West Indies.

The Lesser Antilles are still young land formations and as the recent volcanic eruptions in Montserrat and St. Vincent show, this region continues to grow and re-shape itself. Out of the great expanse of the Atlantic Ocean, the Caribbean came into being as a result of gigantic shifts in the earth's crust. The islands sit atop a plate roughly the size and shape of the Caribbean Sea that is continually pushing up against the larger American Plate. Perched along the edge of this border, the Lesser Antilles were formed by tectonic activity, earthquakes and volcanic eruptions caused by the northward movement of the South American continent.

Although the entire island measures only 616km² (238 sq mi), and is 43km long and 23km wide (27mi by 14mi), it is endowed with a rich geographical diversity. The remarkable contrasts between the island's tropical south and arid north are due to the fact that St. Lucia was actually formed during two different periods of volcanic activity in the eastern Caribbean.

Travelling in the far north and eastern regions of St. Lucia, it is difficult to believe that this is the Caribbean. The open countryside and windblown vegetation seem more reminiscent of some Mediterranean coastlines. Forty million years ago, volcanoes were active and abundant in this area. Other islands in the Lesser Antilles, like Antigua, Barbuda and Marie Galante, also formed at this time. Today, the volcanic mountain ranges of this period are unrecognizable. At the far northern tip of the island, particularly in Cap

Estates, erosion has created a dramatic landscape of isolated rock formations, rounded hilltops and open lowlands.

In the south, St. Lucia's terrain transforms into exotic mountains and forest. The valleys narrow into deep gorges, and hills become sharp ridges towering above the roadside. This is the youngest section of the island. Its creation, along with St. Kitts and Dominica, began 7 million years ago during the latest phase of tectonic activity in the Lesser Antilles. The forces of wind and water have only just begun to make an impression on the landscape.

What remains is some of the most enthralling natural scenery in the West Indies. In the southwest, the magnificent Pitons, **Gros Piton** (798m or 2,618ft) and **Petit Piton** (750m or 2,461ft), rise abruptly from the coastline like two massive cylinders. There is nothing else like them in the Caribbean. St. Lucia's highest peak, **Mount Gimie** (950m or 3,117ft), looms above several forest reserves in the midst of a dense tropical rain forest. The land is steep and rugged, enriched with red and black volcanic soil, and covered with lush green vegetation and fruit trees. Outside Soufrière, the smoldering remains of a collapsed volcano named Qualibou feeds the local spring baths with hot sulfurous water. Between Choiseul and Vieux Fort, in the extreme south, the terrain gradually slopes down from the heights of Mount Grand Magazin to the sea. Here, volcanic outflow has left a layer of extraordinarily fertile soil that has eroded into six deep canyons.

St. Lucia's coastlines reflect the same diversity. Each has its own unique beauty. In the east, the Atlantic shoreline faces the powerful trade winds blowing across the ocean from the northeast. In places like **Grande Anse** and Espérance Bay, the wind has twisted the vegetation and brushed it back from the ocean. Trees grow shaped like surreal figures in the midst of savannah fields and clusters of cacti. All along this coast, rough seas have eroded the shoreline into cliffs, rocky outcrops and isolated stretches of sandy beach. In several places, rivers have deposited large amounts of volcanic sediment and created mangrove swamps.

The west coast is an altogether different landscape. This is the tropical side of St. Lucia. Sheltered from the trade winds and surrounded by the warm Caribbean Sea are sandy beach coves with coconut trees, placid bays and coral reefs.

Fauna and Flora

Fauna

St. Lucia's only indigenous mammal is the agouti. This large rodent, about the size of a house cat, resembles a gerbil with long legs and a tiny tail. Early in the 19th century, the British introduced the Indian mongoose to keep rats from destroying their sugar crops. Watch for a ferret-like creature with a long gray or brown body and a bushy tail darting across a rain forest path. In 1902, Major Cowie of the Royal Engineers left an indelible mark on the island before departing to England, when he decided to release his pet opossums behind his regiment's barracks on Morne Fortune. The manicou, as they are locally known, have since overrun the island. Manicou generally stay in the trees, but because of a weakness for decaying meat and garbage, they are often seen in the vicinity of hotels.

Among the different species of reptiles found in St. Lucia is the boa constrictor, the island's largest snake, which reaches lengths of up to 4m (12ft). In patois, it's called *têtechien*, meaning head of a

Portrait

dog. Once found all over the island, its habitat is now limited to drier areas between Roseau and Canaries and from Marquis to Micoud. Look for its light-brown skin with dark spots along the side in trees or bushes—but don't worry, it's harmless to humans. The St. Lucian viper, or fer de lance, on the other hand, is extremely venomous. These snakes were originally brought to the island by plantation owners who left them in pits around their property to prevent slaves from escaping. Its range is the same as that of the boa, though it prefers coastal areas, particularly the dry scrub and grasslands of the east coast.

The most common reptile, however, is the small gecko or tree lizard, which clings effortlessly to walls or branches. They eat insects or fruit and are absolutely no threat. You may spot the gecko's impressive relative, the iguana, if you hike along the northeast coast. Primarily a tree dweller, it can grow to 2m (6ft) and is recognizable by a pointed ridge along the edge of its spine. There is also the zandoli tere, a

small snake-like lizard that keeps to the ground.

Two extremely rare species, the St. Lucian whiptail lizard and the St. Lucian racer snake inhabit Maria Islands Nature Reserve, off the coast of Vieux Fort. This tiny sanctuary is the only place in the world where they live.

Marine life thrives in the coral reefs and seas surrounding St. Lucia. Among the most exciting developments in the tourism industry here are the growing number of opportunities for wildlife viewing. Each year, between March and July, beaches on the

St. Lucia Parrot

east coast are visited by female sea turtles who lay eggs in the sand. During this period, the St. Lucia Naturalist Society organizes trips to observe this prehistoric ritual and help collect research data. All the Caribbean sea turtles—the loggerhead, the hawksbill, the olive-ridley and the green turtle—can be seen dragging themselves onto the beaches where they themselves were born. The most impressive species, however, is the giant leatherback. One of the largest turtles in the ocean, it can grow up to 2m (6ft) in length and weigh up to 600kg (1,320lbs). An endangered species, the leatherback is threatened by the disappearance of its egg-laying sites as a result of sand mining and the proliferation of beach resorts throughout the Caribbean.

Whale-watching tours provide an opportunity to get close to sperm whales, pilot whales, humpbacks, spotted dolphins, spiner dolphins, fraser dolphins and the playful bottle-nosed dolphin. For divers and snorkellers, below the water surface there are octopi, moray eels and seahorses. Queen angelfish, blue tangs, sergeant major and parrot fish are some of the tropical fish swimming around exotic coral formations in St. Lucia.

Bird-watchers will find many different varieties to add to their sighting lists. The island's most famous bird, the St. Lucia parrot, or *jacquot* in patois, is most often seen flying above the tree canopy in the rain forest. Once considered a delicacy by Creoles, it was nearly wiped out due to overhunting. In 1980, the government finally introduced legislation to protect them in the wild. Education programs and enthusiastic public support has changed the situation dramatically

and now the parrot is flourishing.

From the coast, brown pelicans can be seen gliding just above the water, at any moment plunging in head first to scoop up fish in their expandable bills. At greater heights, the magnificent frigate bird soars gracefully with its pointed or forked tail and huge wingspan, often reaching 2.5m (7.5ft) across. Although Frigate Islands Nature Reserve near Dennery is set aside as a nesting site, frigate birds are seen all along St. Lucia's coastline.

Reddish egrets and several types of herons, such as the green heron, frequent riverbeds and tidal flat areas. One of the island's few raptors is the broad-winged hawk, a large, brown bird with a white belly. Keep your binoculars handy to catch the quick movements of a purple throated hummingbird and the antillean crested hummingbird, or watch for the black and orange St. Lucian oriole or the yellow breasted bananaquit.

Flora

The vibrant colours typically used by St. Lucia's artists are inspired by the trees and flowers that surround them. The calabash,

St. Lucia's national tree, produces gourd-like fruits that are used to make bowls and cups. Its purple and yellow flowers open only one night a year, when they are pollinated by bats. One of the more common pine trees is the blue mahoe. Introduced from Jamaica in the 1950s, it was planted in large numbers in deforested areas to prevent soil erosion. Local artisans use the red and black seeds of the dedefonden tree, called "donkey eyes," to make necklaces and earrings, which are seen in craft shops. The bois canon is another common tree, similar in appearance to the smaller papaya tree, but without the fruit. It has a solid trunk that grows up to 25m (75ft) high and is sparsely covered by hollow branches and large leaves. Along hiking trails, the mammoth chatagnier is an impressive sight. Often reaching heights above 30m (90ft) and 3m (9ft) in diameter, they are supported by giant claw-like root systems sometimes as thick as 1 to 2m (3 to 6ft).

Hibiscus

Beneath St. Lucia's tall palm trees and bright bougainvillea is an abundance of stunning tropical flowers. There is the purple heliconia, orchids, and the anthurium, a distinctive heart-shaped red flower. Hummingbirds are attracted to the aromatic blossoms of the frangipani and the vibrant colors of allamanda, ixora and balisier.

History

Indigenous Peoples in the Caribbean

Before Europeans arrived in the Caribbean, the region extending from the tip of the Bahamas to Trinidad was populated by approximately 5 million indigenous people. How they lived remains much of a mystery. They left few records of their civilization and so much of what we know about them is taken from European accounts. Three waves of immigration populated the region.

The first inhabitants of the Caribbean were the **Ciboney**. They originated in southern Florida before migrating to the Bahamas around 2000 BC and then later into the Greater Antilles. They established themselves on the north-western tip of Cuba and Hispaniola.

The **Arawak** followed much later, around 300 BC, coming from the Orinoco basin in northeastern South America. They were able to settle as far as Haiti and Cuba and even the Bahamas. By AD 1500, they were living mainly in the Greater Antilles, having absorbed or killed off the Ciboney in their path.

The name Arawak was created by modern scholars. These people identified themselves instead with the island on which they lived. The Arawak lived in coastal villages, sustaining themselves on seafood, hunting and agriculture. Food was plentiful and the tropical climate meant finding shelter posed few problems. They practiced a form of slash and burn agriculture called *conuco*, which involved burning away the forest, heaping the soil into mounds and enriching it with ashes. They farmed a variety of fruits and vegetables but their most important crop was bitter yucca, from which cassava bread was made. Yucca provided them with a major source of sugar and starch.

The last group of indigenous people to enter the Caribbean were the **Carib**, who came from northeastern South America about AD 1000. They mainly inhabited the Lesser Antilles and the northwestern tip of Trinidad. When the Spanish arrived, the Caribs were encroaching on the Arawak in eastern Puerto Rico. The Carib practiced the same *conuco* agriculture and were expert boatbuilders, but were generally less technologically advanced than the Arawak. They were fewer in numbers and their society was more warlike, although their reputation for violence and cruelty, including cannibalism, was probably exaggerated by Europeans. Carib peoples generally received Europeans with generosity until they were attacked or deceived.

Today there are only 3,000 indigenous peoples, mostly Caribs of mixed-blood, left in the Caribbean. Most live on reservations in Dominica and St. Vincent.

The Age of Discovery

Today, we have come to view the voyage of Christopher Columbus from two radically different perspectives. One celebrates the discovery of the Americas as a beginning, the other mourns the beginning of the end. But there is no doubting the significance of this event in world history.

Who knows if Columbus would have appreciated the irony of his legacy? Columbus set out to find a shorter trade route to the Far East and died convinced he had accomplished his goal by landing in the Indies. His first accomplishment, however, was to persuade the king and queen of Spain to sponsor an expedition to the unknown. In 1492, he led three ships, the *Pinta*, the *Santa Maria* and the *Nina*, out of Spain to the Canary Islands and then caught the northeast trade winds across the Atlantic. After 36 days at sea, they landed in San Salvador in the Bahamas and then continued along the northeast coast of Cuba and Hispaniola (present day Haiti and the Dominican Republic). On December 26, 1492, before returning to Spain, Columbus left 39 men on the north coast of Haiti to build La Navidad, the first European settlement in the New World.

The voyage was considered a success and the Spanish monarchy readily outfitted Columbus with enough soldiers and provisions to establish permanent settlements. A year later, 17 ships embarked on a three-year journey through the Greater Antilles and the Leewards as far south as Dominica. La Navidad was found deserted, its rough shelters burned to the ground. It took several years before a successful settlement could be built, Columbus being a seaman rather than an administrator. Not until 1496, when Columbus's brother Bartholomew founded Santo Domingo on the southeast coast of Hispaniola, was Spain able to anchor itself firmly in the New World.

The gold Columbus found on earlier voyages lured him farther south in 1498 with a smaller expedition that reached Trinidad. At this time, the motivation for exploration also became intertwined with the growing demand for slave labour among Spanish settlers. When Columbus undertook his final voyage in 1502, through the Lesser Antilles to the Caribbean coast of Central America, he made only brief stops at several Windward Islands, including Martinique. Finding no gold, Columbus saw no reason to stay longer than necessary to capture indigenous slaves and replenish water supplies.

From the beginning, colonial expansion in the Caribbean had a devastating impact on the indigenous population. The discovery of gold in the Americas created a focus for the Spanish, who depended on a steady supply of indigenous people to work as slaves in the mines and fields of its conquered territories. After their capture, they were organized into *encomiendas*, a brutal system of forced labour, distributed amongst colonial officials and then simply worked to death. Harsh treatment, malnourishment and, above all, European diseases, killed them quickly and in great numbers. One by one, entire island communities were wiped out.

The age of exploration in the Caribbean was followed in the 16th century by vigorous efforts to settle the new colonial territories. Although settlement expanded across the Greater Antilles, particularly in Cuba and Hispaniola, Spain's interest in the region began to focus on exploiting its more lucrative possessions on the mainland. During this period, the Lesser Antilles remained largely unexplored except as a source of indigenous slaves. Eventually Spain's indifference to these islands led other European powers, notably the British, French and Dutch, to establish their own territorial claims in the region. As the Caribs vanished from each of the islands, with the exception of St. Vincent and Dominica, these territories were usurped by a new

wave of European settlement.

Early Settlement of the Lesser Antilles

Portrait

Throughout the 16th century, Spain continued as the dominant force in the New World, reaping unprecedented wealth from its conquests of the Inca and Aztec empires on the mainland. Flotillas, huge convoys full of booty bound for Spain, were prime targets for the bands of pirates and privateers that roamed the Caribbean Sea. They knew the islands extremely well, in many cases operating as mercenary forces for Britain or France. The legend of El Dorado, which referred to a city of gold somewhere between Venezuela and northern Brazil, had led to several European settlements along the "Wild Coast" of Guyana. The Lesser Antilles only began to interest the British, French and Dutch when raids on these settlements forced them to realize their colonial ambitions elsewhere.

The arrival of the first tobacco crop in England from Virginia in 1613 changed the course of Caribbean history. Now European investors began to appreciate that overseas agricul tural colonies could be profitable and self-supporting. Instead of funding privateers to raid Spanish ships and ports, capital was channelled into large-scale colonial settlements that would provide tobacco and other tropical products for the European market. Unlike other colonial enterprises in North America, the prime motivation for settling the Caribbean was profit.

meant colonization efforts were initially focused on unoccupied islands. In the 1620s, the British established the first successful agricultural settlements in St. Kitts and Barbados.

Barbados rapidly became an immensely prosperous colony, exporting a variety of crops, especially tobacco, back to the mother country and encouraging investors to expand the development of the island. The French followed later in 1635 with their own agriculturally based colonies in Guadeloupe and Martinique, but they were hindered by Carib attacks. The massacre of a British settlement by Caribs in St. Lucia in 1639 persuaded the British to abandon attempts to settle other islands in the Lesser Antilles.

Although many of the indigenous communities in the eastern Caribbean had been exterminated by the Spanish, the remaining Caribs survived by retreating to the more mountainous interiors of the Lesser Antilles. In 1605 the *Olive Branch*, an English ship on its way to Guyana, landed on St. Lucia at Vieux Fort. Of the 67 persons who disembarked on the island, only 19 were alive five weeks later. The persistent threat of Carib attacks

The first colonists in the Caribbean endured great difficulties. Many died while crossing the Atlantic in crowded ships with minimal food supplies. They arrived in a strange new land lacking the knowledge or experience to deal with the tropical climate. A small percentage of the colonists were wealthy merchants or nobles but most of colonial society at this time was made up of indentured white servants. In exchange for three to five years of labour and limited personal rights, a master provided them with food, shelter and clothing and at the end of the contract they received freedom dues in the form of capital or land.

The early settlers were mainly inexperienced farmers with few resources. The high cost of European goods forced them to adopt Carib food, housing and agricultural practices for survival. Land clearance was a slow, arduous process, so it took many years of hard labour before colonists could rise above very primitive living conditions.

French settlement of the Caribbean began in 1625 with an expedition to St. Kitts, creating a base for future colonial expansion. The first wave of colonialists soon moved to Guadeloupe and Hispaniola in 1635 and then Martinique. Unlike the British model of leasing islands out to wealthy merchants, French colonization was based on state directives and the formation of official companies that operated as monopolies. Two ministers were instrumental in the development of French colonial policy: Cardinal Richelieu in the 1620s and Jean-Baptiste Colbert in the 1660s. Labour shortages led to the recruitment of *enga-gés*, indentured servants, to clear land and work the fields. Although the French settlements developed slowly, they were eventually able to expand their presence to Dominica, St. Lucia and even as far south as Grenada.

By 1645, all the islands in the Lesser Antilles were claimed by the French, English or Dutch. Now with a growing population of free servants looking for land, governments had an eager supply of new settlers. As the last refuges of the Carib tribes in the region were being encroached upon, confrontations increased, slowing development in St. Lucia, Dominica, Guadeloupe and St.Vincent. The decades of prosperity in St. Kitts and Barbados came to a halt in the early 1640s, when the value of tobacco dropped as a result of increased exports from Virginia flooding the European market. There was a brief period of economic difficulty until sugar cane was planted in Barbados, an event that would have a revolutionary impact on Caribbean society and ultimately the world.

The economic vacuum created by falling tobacco prices was quickly filled by the production of sugar cane on a massive scale. The hot tropical climate of the Caribbean was ideal for its cultivation. Originally, the plantation system was used by the Dutch in Brazil who offered capital loans, supplies and later slaves to planters in Barbados to run their expanding operations. European demand for sugar soared and in the absence of any significant competition, Barbados became the wealthiest colony in the British Empire.

The enormous economic changes introduced by sugar cane were surpassed by its social impact on West Indian society. The cultivation of sugar cane is an extremely labour intensive task. As the plantations expanded, so did the need for more workers. In the beginning, the available pool of white indentured servants sufficed. However since most of these workers emigrated at the end of their tenure to other less developed islands in search of their own land, this system only provided a temporary labour force. Plantation owners searched for ways to solve the problem of labour shortages. A solution was found by importing thousands of African slaves to the region. Within two decades, they had replaced white labourers. Not only were they a cheap source of labour, they were also able to adapt more efficiently to the climate and diseases of the Caribbean environment.

The Push for Colonial Territorial Expansion

Throughout the 17th century, Barbados continued as the centre of economic activity in the Caribbean. Shipping routes from Europe concentrated on transporting sugar out of Barbados, and any available capital that could have been used to finance other settlement enterprises was instead invested in the lucrative sugar industry. As a result, most of the other Windward Islands were largely ignored. They were considered wild and remote, a perspective reinforced by the persistent efforts of local Caribs to repel European encroachments on their land. For many decades, attempts to settle these islands were limited to military expeditions and small garrison communities.

In 1651, the French undertook the first substantial attempt to settle St. Lucia since the massacre of an English settlement by the local Caribs 11 years earlier. The expedition was commanded by an officer from Martinique named De Rousselan. Because of extensive experience in the Caribbean and marriage to a Carib woman, he was able to maintain a peaceful relationship with the locals.

The "White Man's Graveyard"

Europeans feared the Caribbean for a very long time. The ports and settlements of the New World were a breeding ground for diseases like smallpox, tuberculosis, yellow fever and malaria. Since death by disease was the most likely outcome of a visit to this region, the Caribbean soon gained a reputation as the "white man's graveyard."

The loss of life was indeed staggering. Epidemics spread rapidly in the close-quartered communities of the small islands, killing soldiers, slaves and settlers. One in three slaves died during their first two years in the West Indies, while three out of four Europeans perished soon after their arrival. Heightened demands from plantation owners for additional slave labour couple with a stronger natural immunity against yellow fever and the severest strains of malaria led to a massive-scale importation of slaves. This explains how the Caribbean came to be repopulated with Africans.

A fort was built and the colony successfully cultivated several crops. When Governor De Rousselan died in 1654, his successors were beset by disease, Carib aggressions and a series of British incursions. In 1664, a combined force of British soldiers and Carib reinforcements from Barbados took St. Lucia from the French. The British stationed 1,000 men to defend the island but two years later disease had taken all but 89.

The Peace of Breda, signed in 1667, handed St. Lucia back to France but repeated British protests eventually resulted in the island being given neutral status until the issue could be resolved. The predominantly French and Irish population continued to develop St. Lucia without interference until the beginning of the 18th century.

The commercial success of Barbados encouraged the governments of France and

England to assert territorial claims in the Lesser Antilles. A long period of intense military conflict ensued while both nations invaded Carib strongholds and fought one another for ownership of several islands. In their attempts to take control of Grenada, Martinique, Guadeloupe and Dominica, French armies struggled to subdue Carib inhabitants. In some cases, resistance was so fierce that commanders relented only after most of the island's indigenous population had been exterminated. In 1660, a peace treaty was put forward by the governor-general of the French islands, Philippe de Lonvillers de Poincy, which ended hostilities by granting the Caribs rights to Dominica and St. Vincent.

The colonial rivalry that dominated the Caribbean in the 18th century reflected events in Europe and North America. St. Lucia, in particular, took on immense significance in the context of the wars raging between France and England. The degree of interest in the island may seem disproportionate considering its minimal resources, but control of St. Lucia had important strategic value. Wars in the Caribbean were fought almost exclusively at sea since few islands in the Lesser Antilles had any permanent garrisons. A col-

ony's fate was therefore often determined by its access to naval reinforcements. Castries is one of the best harbours in the West Indies. A wide sheltered bay with deep water, it was prized by naval commanders because they could gather large fleets in one location. More importantly, however, ships moored along the island's west coast, in places like Pigeon Island or Marigot Bay, could monitor activity at Fort Royal, Martinique, France's largest naval garrison in the region. For this reason, both countries looked upon possession of the tiny island of St. Lucia as critical to the defense of their colonial empires.

St. Lucia passed between the English and French 14 times before the issue of sovereignty was finally resolved in 1814. Most of these exchanges were the result of diplomatic negotiations rather than ground wars on Lucian soil. It was common practice among the various European powers to use colonial possessions as bargaining pieces during peace talks in order to preserve their territorial integrity on the continent. Changes in sovereignty, even after armed conflict, were not necessarily catastrophic events. One of the reasons for attacking an island was to gain control of its valuable sugar crop. A century earlier, conquering armies normally destroyed settlements but this strategy changed as sugar prices rose in Europe. In the 18th century, commanders were instead instructed to leave the island's infrastructure intact, especially its sugar plantations and appease the local population to ensure production would continue.

In 1763, the Treaty of Paris ended the Seven Years War, which had been fought not only in Europe but also on the Caribbean Sea. In the aftermath, Britain returned Martinique and Guadeloupe to France in exchange for Canada, Grenada, Dominica, St. Vincent and Tobago. After intense debate, Britain reluctantly agreed to hand St. Lucia over to the French. Following the treaty, St. Lucia received an influx of French and Irish settlers who eventually created an administrative framework for the island and laid the foundation for greater development.

The War of American Independence (1775-1783) once again pitted Britain and France against each other. The alliance between the American revolutionaries and the French expanded the conflict to the sugar-producing islands of the Caribbean. The British now faced a much stronger French naval force under the command of admirals

Choiseul and de Grasse, losing most of their possessions in the Lesser Antilles, except for Barbados, Antigua and St. Lucia. At the Battle of the Saints in 1782, a British fleet under Admiral Rodney, stationed in St. Lucia, surprised and defeated a French fleet bound for an attack on Jamaica. In spite of this big loss, France emerged the victor when war ended in 1783 with the Treaty of Versailles. In the Caribbean, the islands reverted to the pre-war status quo. St. Lucia returned to France and the American colonies gained their independence from Britain.

The last period of military conflict in the Windwards was precipitated by the French Revolution in 1789. The extreme political turmoil that gripped France following the execution of King Louis XVI generated tremendous anxiety among the white planter classes in the French West Indies. They feared the new Republican regime would revoke their property rights to redistribute the land of their sugar estates and abolish slavery. A revolutionary tribunal arrived in St. Lucia in 1792, led by a Republican zealot named La Crosse who used the guillotine against Royalists. The island soon degenerated into anarchy as plantations were abandoned and destroyed

The Brigands Story

The many bands of runaway slaves that existed throughout the Caribbean dispels the notion of Africans as submissive captives. During the era of slavery in St. Lucia, slaves established camps hidden deep in the interior of the island. Certainly, many attempted to escape, but they also used other more subtle forms of rebellion against their masters, like working slowly or not reproducing. In Jamaica, runaway slaves called "maroons" waged a full-scale armed rebellion for their freedom and, in St. Lucia, there were the Brigand Wars.

When Republican forces in France overthrew the monarchy and assumed power, they intended to destroy the old order. On February 24, 1794, the new Republican government issued a decree granting freedom to all slaves in the French colonies. The capture of St. Lucia by British forces in 1794, however, annulled this radical piece of legislation. The British government had no intentions of upsetting the profitable plantation system by removing its chief source of labour. It wasn't until much later, in 1838, that emancipation became a reality for slaves in the British colonies.

With the prospect of continued slavery under British rule, many slaves took to the forests and were soon joined by Republican supporters and a few French soldiers. Aided by Republican agents from Guadeloupe, they formed armed units for the purpose of destabilizing the island and defeating the British. An intense guerrilla war ensued against the occupational forces and French Royalist planters who cooperated with the British authorities in order to maintain their estates and to preserve the system of slavery from which they profited.

The British commanders called them "brigands." From a network of strategic strongholds around the island, which included observation posts, tunnels and caves, the brigands mounted a very successful military campaign that lasted almost four years. Their raiding activities created chaos, with all but a few estates having their crops and buildings burned to the ground.

After a decisive brigand victory at the Battle of Rabot in 1795, British control loosened considerably, until their soldiers eventually retreated the night before a major offensive against their forces on the Morne. St. Lucia was controlled by the brigands for a year until the arrival of a large British force regained possession of Pigeon Island, Vigie and Morne Fortune. The Brigand War continued for another two years as the British fought to expand their authority to the interior of the island. By November 1797, the brigands relinquished their arms according to the terms of a negotiated ceasefire. Many ultimately gained their freedom and served as soldiers for the British colonial forces in regiments in the West Indies and Africa.

by slaves and Republican supporters.

The response from white planters in Martinique and Guadeloupe was to seek military protection from Britain to preserve their colonial estates. Subsequently, a large British force arrived in St. Lucia, capturing the main garrison at Morne Fortune. Bands of slaves and loyal Republicans, called "Brigands," escaped to the hinterland areas and mounted a guerrilla campaign against British rule. This "Guerre de Brigands" was put down within a year and the island experienced a short period of relative calm. That lasted until the Treaty of Armiens in 1802 when St. Lucia was returned to France, only to have it taken back by the British a year later.

The issue of sovereignty was finally resolved in 1814 by the Treaty of Paris, which made Britain's *de facto* control of the island official. Over a century of continuous political instability had severely limited St. Lucia's development and prevented large scale settlement. A new colonial administration was formed and the island entered a period of economic growth and prosperity as forests were cleared for sugar production.

Slavery in the Caribbean

Caribbean slaves fared much worse than those in North America. The living conditions and labour demands for a slave varied from one island to the next, but life was extremely difficult all over the region, and it was even harder as a field worker on a sugar plantation.

In the early years of sugar production in the 17th century, planters essentially treated their slaves as renewable units of labour. The incredibly high mortality rate among slaves was caused mainly by malnourishment and disease. Birth rates were consequently also very low so planters simply depended on buying new slaves to replace those who died. After the importation of slaves to the British West Indies was abolished in the 19th century, there was a general shift to improve living conditions, not necessarily for humanitarian reasons but out of an economic need to preserve a valuable labour force.

On the plantations, slaves struggled to survive with very little assistance from their masters. In the Windwards, a section of land was set aside for them to grow their own food. Housing was usually a small one- or two-room mud and straw hut situated far away from the master's home. They cooked their meals, made their own clothing and entertained themselves. Hunger and malnourishment were persistent problems. A lack of adequate protein in their diet combined with 12- to 16-hour days of hard labour in the fields made slaves particularly vulnerable to disease and illness.

By the 19th century when sugar production peaked in the Caribbean, Africans constituted more than 95% of the Caribbean population. On any given estate, eight or nine white managers controlled several hundred Africans. It was only a matter of time before slaves assumed a much broader role in colonial society as carpenters, masons, sailors, domestic servants and skilled artisans.

Emancipation

Emancipation was by far the most important event in the British West Indies in the 19th century. The campaigns for abolition in Great Britain exposed the darker aspects of Caribbean society. The British government was confronted with two seemingly irreconcilable concerns in relation to the issue of slavery. More than any other colonial empire in the West Indies, the British islands had concentrated on sugar production. They had prospered enormously but this wealth depended on slave labour. When abolitionists protested against institutionalized slavery, planters on all the islands resisted, fearing the end of a very lucrative and comfortable way of life.

The eradication of slavery in the Caribbean was achieved in stages. Leaders of the abolitionist movement recognized the ability of the powerful planter classes to prevent island assemblies from passing emancipation legislation. The first step for abolitionists was to enact legislation that the British government had the authority to enforce. Their tactic was to pursue a ban on the slave trade since maritime commerce fell under London's jurisdiction.

Thus, in 1808, the commercial practice of purchasing slaves in Africa and shipping them across the ocean for sale in the New World was finally made illegal. A slave registry law, introduced in 1820, made it impossible for new slaves to be smuggled into the colonies and provided a means of holding masters accountable for their treatment of slaves. This marked a radical departure from past policies in the British West Indies. For the first time, planters no longer enjoyed total control over their slaves without state interference.

Church leaders and their congregations were some of the most dynamic forces behind the abolitionist movement in Britain and the Caribbean. A wave of Methodist and Baptist missionaries arrived in the West Indies to convert slaves and to provide moral support and organizational strength to their cause. In England, support for emancipation was gaining enormous strength; so much so, that by 1823, the British government committed itself to ending slavery.

The next stage of the abolition campaign was to ameliorate the working conditions of slaves. A set of laws was introduced in the 1820s that substantially increased their rights and improved their working conditions. A slave owner's right to punish a slave was restricted, the unity of a slave family was protected, field work was abolished on Sundays and the right to congregate for religious worship was assured.

In spite of the political pressure put on the British government to abolish slavery, it was ultimately events in the Caribbean that forced legislators to act. The end of the slave trade had created a serious labour shortage on the sugar plantations. Low reproduction rates among slaves compounded the problem. The general response from planters was to work their slaves even harder to maintain production.

In 1831, thousands of slaves in Jamaica, led by Sam Sharpe, a Baptist preacher, mounted a rebellion that devastated several areas of the island. The Baptist Wars were repressed with uncommon severity by British soldiers and colonial militia. Reports of how savagely the slaves had been treated soon reached Britain, sparking public outrage. The British government responded to the intense political pressure by enacting the Abolition Act of 1833.

This legislation provided for a transition period until 1838, when all slaves in the British West Indies would be freed.

Post-Emancipation and the Colonial Period

For over two centuries, slaves had been under the control of a master who forced them to do monotonous, back-breaking physical labour for his profit. Few slaves had ever known any other way of life. Suddenly, the structure of Caribbean society was radically and fundamentally transformed. Although it represented a moral victory for the British Empire, emancipation created enormous problems for colonial administrators. Imagine the difficulties for a small island colony, like St. Lucia, when suddenly 80% of its population is no longer under the "care" of an individual and now requires public services, employment and land.

Colonial governments were ill-prepared to deal with the complexities of the situation. In the past, island legislatures had mainly concerned themselves with the needs of white plantation owners, a very small, privileged portion of the population. Planters dominated these assemblies and used their influence to protect the specific interests of the sugar industry. The immediate impact of emancipation was to increase the cost of production simply because workers now had to be paid wages. Thus colonial leaders faced a sudden increase in the population under their jurisdiction and in demands for public services, while island revenues were beginning to fall drastically.

During this period, the sugar industry in the British West Indies experienced another great setback from which it never recovered. In 1846, London introduced legislation eliminating duties on sugar imports from outside the British West Indies. Caribbean planters could no longer depend on access to a protected British market. They were now forced to compete with other sugar producers in the United States and Cuba which still used slave labour. Moreover, St. Lucia's uneven terrain prevented cultivation on a scale large enough to compete effectively without a source of cheap labour. Ultimately, the rise in labour costs and reduced prices for sugar led many planters to abandon their estates and leave the islands.

In St. Lucia, approximately 18,000 slaves were freed. Their lives were no longer controlled by or dependent on a plantation master. Most freed slaves were determined to find their own small plots of land where they could live independently. Working the fields of the plantation had given them the farming skills to grow their own food as well as other crops, like bananas, cocoa and nutmeg for sale at local markets or for export. Compared to Barbados and St. Kitts, St. Lucia still had large tracts of unoccupied land that freed slaves could rent or purchase. Nonetheless, those areas best suited for agriculture were owned by the plantations, which meant that free slaves began to occupy marginal lands. In the more rugged parts of the island, squatters took over vacant Crown land.

The end of slavery, however, did not lead to the creation of a more democratic and equitable society in the British West Indies. The racial divisions of slavery were reincarnated in the form of rigid socioeconomic divisions within the population. In every respect, St. Lucian society continued to be dominated by the white planter class. Their immense landholdings and connections to British government and high society provided them with economic and political power.

An emerging force in Caribbean society, however, were the population of mulattoes, or Creoles, who by British law were born free. In many cases, they became wealthy landowners, professionals, merchants and, later, academics. They generally aspired to British cultural values and sensibilities, but Creoles still encountered a great deal of discrimination among the island's elite white population. As more and more planters abandoned their estates and returned to Britain, it would be the Creoles who took over civil administration and eventually, political office. The vast majority of the population, however, was composed of black peasants who sustained themselves by farming small plots of land and working for short periods on large plantations. Most rented their land from white or Creole planters at relatively high rates and received low wages for field labour. It was a meagre living that left no money for education or the means to improve their situation.

The decline of the West Indian sugar industry relegated small island colonies like St. Lucia to the bottom of the British government's priority list. As a result, the development of the Windward colonies continued to suffer because of inadequate infrastructure and ineffective administrators. Colonial officials and administrators were appointed by the Crown in England and the West Indies became a dumping ground for inept colonial officials and unqualified English aristocrats. They often arrived without previous experience in the Caribbean and certainly without enough background knowledge of the societies they were expected to lead. Generally, the ruling classes never fully embraced the island colonies as their home. Instead, they maintained a very close connection to the mother country with only a detached interest in the problems of black peasants. Moreover, the island's ruling classes, rooted in a plantation economy, lacked the will or expertise to adapt to a new reality.

In 1898, St. Lucia and Trinidad became the first Crown colonies in the West Indies. While other colonies, like Canada and Australia, had evolved into independent, democratic countries, the British government implemented a more authoritarian style of government in the Windwards. Hitherto, a governor appointed by the British government under the direction of its Colonial Office had supreme control over the island's affairs. The desperate state of affairs in St. Lucia convinced the Colonial Office the planters were incapable of governing the island. There was also strong resistance to black majority rule from both the planters and the British government.

The institution of a governor did little to change the status quo in St. Lucia. The lack of attention devoted to developing the island's economy and public services was due to neglect at the top levels of government. By choosing to bring in foreigners to run the colony, the British government ultimately curtailed the advancement of local blacks and Creoles into administrative positions. It was a policy that kept those who were most informed about what problems needed to be addressed in a powerless position; and more importantly, individuals with a heartfelt interest in improving conditions on the island were prevented from doing so.

In the economic sphere, a dangerous ambivalence typified colonial policy. There was a deeply ingrained attitude among high-ranking colonial officials that the economies of smaller West Indian islands could only be based on agricultural production. Despite falling sugar prices and heightened competition from larger producers such as Cuba, no comprehensive initiatives were ever undertaken to diversify St. Lucia's economy. That narrow understanding of the island's potential ultimately discouraged the type of entrepreneurship that could have broadened economic opportunities. Without an industrial sector of its own, St. Lucia was forced to import expensive manufactured goods from England.

By the First World War, living conditions had become intolerable for the black majority. Decades of economic stagnation had resulted in very limited growth and few opportunities for those outside the very small circle of elites on the island. Meanwhile, the black population struggled with chronic unemployment and government neglect in the areas of public education and health. In this context, the extreme disparities that pervaded colonial society in the British West Indies would inevitably lead to a period of widespread unrest across the region.

Early 20th Century

For black soldiers of the British West Indies Regiment, the experience of serving overseas in the First World War awakened a determination to increase their political rights at home. Islanders made immense sacrifices for the

Crown. St. Lucia lost 36 men. Throughout the 1920s, political life in the Windward Islands came to be dominated by protests for improvements in welfare services and constitutional reforms to give black and Creole persons a more influential role in colonial government. A long tradition of forming associations and unions to represent economic interests to the Crown provided the vehicle for a growing political consciousness among black workers and middle-class Creoles.

The Great Depression proved to be a huge catalyst for political activity in the eastern Caribbean. St. Lucia's dependence on sugar made it extremely vulnerable to economic disaster. As demand and prices for sugar plummeted, the government's budget shrank, forcing it to eliminate many public works programs. Before long, soaring unemployment levels and starvation diets galvanized public dissatisfaction with colonial rule. In this volatile environment, union leaders were able to strengthen their positions as representatives of the people's interests. They organized strikes and demonstrations across the Windwards, pressing for self-government and increased workers' rights. Coal carriers and sugar workers in St.

Lucia went on strike seeking higher wages and regulations designed to protect them in the workplace. On other islands, such as Jamaica, Trinidad and Barbados, riots ended in massive property damage and many deaths.

The threat of increasing violence and instability prompted the British government to investigate the source of the disturbances. In 1940, Lord Moyne presented a report on the current problems facing the British Caribbean and made policy recommendations. Essentially, the report called for democratic reforms to allow islanders greater electoral representation in the legislative councils and access to higher-ranking administrative positions. Moyne also emphasized the need to make more land accessible to small farmers and improve conditions for workers. In response, the British government made funds and grants available to the islands for public works to curb high unemployment and health programs to reduce malnutrition and disease.

Independence

The policy recommendations put forward by the Moyne Report represented an important victory for union leaders. During this period, the unions emerged as the most important source of political power in the eastern Caribbean. The report's conclusions reinforced the British Crown's growing support for self-government in the West Indies. Clearly, the wheels were in motion for making independence a reality for the Windward Islands. But the momentum in the Colonial Office was stalled by the outbreak of war in Europe.

In the immediate post-war period, Great Britain faced pressure to grant its colonies around the world self-government. Underlying the Crown's philosophy, however, was a firm belief in an evolutionary approach to independence in the West Indies. St. Lucia received universal adult suffrage in 1951. By 1956, all of the Windward colonies achieved "Associated Status" in the British Commonwealth. This essentially put the responsibility of government in the hands of elected representatives. Shortly after, in conjunction with the British government, island politicians united all 10 Caribbean territories under the West Indies Federation. For many of the smaller, less developed islands, like St. Lucia, it was considered a necessary step before independence because it provided

them with a more influential political voice and a stronger bargaining position in dealings with multinational corporations operating in the Caribbean. Unfortunately, the federation collapsed in 1962, when Trinidad and Jamaica decided they were unwilling to support the poorer Windward Islands.

The Moyne Report was also a significant economic catalyst. The steady deterioration of the sugar industry in St. Lucia and throughout the eastern Caribbean created a severe unemployment problem. Widespread unrest alerted the British government of the need to search for a new source of revenue that could provide income for small farmers as well as plantation owners. Bananas were introduced and gradually took over as the island's largest export. In the 1960s, production expanded with the help of colonial subsidies and protected access to the U.K. market. Bananas solved the problem of unemployment in St. Lucia but the pattern of overdependence on a single crop was repeated, leaving the island just as vulnerable to changes in the marketplace as it had previously been.

St. Lucia gained its independence in 1979. The last two decades have been dominated by significant changes in the island's economy. The once strong banana market has been shaken by international events. Recent protests from the World Trade Organization have led to the elimination of British subsidies to the island's banana industry and another period of economic upheaval. Now St. Lucia is confronting the enormous socioeconomic challenge of making the transition from bananas to tourism.

Politics

Lucian government is modelled on the British form of parliamentary democracy. The head of state is a constitutional monarch, Queen Elizabeth II, who is represented on the island by a governor-general. The people are represented by 17 elected members in the House of Assembly and in the senate chamber by 11 nominated members.

Political life for the masses in St. Lucia began in 1951 with the introduction of universal adult suffrage. By this time, independence movements had taken root in the Caribbean but the British government preferred a gradual transition by granting the island "associated statehood" in 1964 and then independence in 1979.

The two major rivals in Lucian politics are the United Workers Party (UWP) and the St. Lucia Labour Party (SLP). On the surface, St. Lucia's political spectrum seems limited to Marxist variations; yet it represents a tendency among Caribbean political parties to identify themselves with the labour movement. The connection, however, is generally historical and not necessarily ideological.

The groundwork for St. Lucia's political culture lay in trade unionism. Out of the desperate economic conditions of the 1930s, labour unions gained immense strength in the Caribbean. Unions were magnets for those seeking to change the status quo and they soon became mass movements attracting skilled professionals as well as unskilled workers. In the postwar period, Lucian society was still controlled by a foreign power and a small racial elite. In this context, unions were perceived as the only credible organizations representing the interests of the common people. They provided leadership, funds, and later votes to island reformers working for greater autonomy from Britain. During the early stages of self-government, when political parties were being formed, Lucian society was largely made up of agricultural workers and small farmers, so the transition from labour union to labour party was not only natural, it was also necessary for political power.

For over 30 years, the more conservative UWP, led by Sir John Compton, dominated Lucian politics. A former lawyer, Compton led the country through its most important stages of political development as chief minister in 1964 and then as prime minister in 1979. After a short absence from power, from 1979 to 1982, he returned as prime minister until the UWP's electoral defeat in 1997 to the SLP.

A sour mix of cynicism and willingness for change on the part of voters expressed itself in the SLP's winning 16 of 17 seats in the House of Assembly in the 1997 election. The new majority government, headed by Kenny Anthony, assumed power with a mandate to diversify the economy and reduce unemployment. So far, SLP policies reflect the contradictions of Tony Blair's New Labour in Britain. Prime Minister Anthony's approach to St. Lucia's formidable economic challenges has been to maintain most State-owned enterprises while showing a decidedly pro-business attitude to stimulate foreign

investment and generate economic growth.

In foreign relations, the need for a stronger voice in world affairs and a recognition of common interests has involved St. Lucia in several efforts at regional integration. In 1973, the Caribbean Community (CARICOM) united Caribbean commonwealth states to promote economic integration among its members and to act as a supporting agency for maintaining adequate standards of health and education services. Achieving consensus has always been a difficult objective among the many diverse nations of the Caribbean. One major source of division within CARICOM that is hindering its effectiveness are the huge economic disparities between members like Jamaica and St. Vincent. To tackle issues with a narrower geographic focus, St. Lucia joined the Organization of Eastern Caribbean States (OECS) in 1981 along with Antigua and Barbuda, Dominica, Grenada, Montserrat, St. Kitts and Nevis, St. Vincent and the Grenadines. Today the OECS is taking on an increasingly important role, particularly in the sphere of natural resource management and the development of regional trade programs.

Portrait

Economy

Up until the mid 20th century, St. Lucia's economy was dominated by the sugar industry. The pattern of dependence on a single crop was established during the early stages of colonization. Large sugar plantations occupied the most fertile areas of the island and no efforts were made to diversify the economy. By the 1950s, falling sugar prices and competition from larger, more efficient producers like Cuba had created an economic crisis across the Windward Islands. The British Colonial Office desperately searched for an alternative source of income for both poor small farmers and estate owners.

A solution was achieved in the late 1950s with the large-scale introduction of bananas. Unlike sugar cane, bananas could be planted on almost any type of terrain, including the steep marginal areas where most small farmers owned land.

Bananas

Because of St. Lucia's colonial status, farmers were also given protected access to the British market and prices were subsidized. By 1965, bananas surpassed sugar to form 90% of the island's exports.

Bananas were such a profitable venture that they came to be called the "green gold" of the Caribbean. In spite of their value, however, there are pitfalls. The tall, top-heavy plants are easily uprooted by high winds and when storms hit, the result can be devastating. After Hurricane Debbie struck St. Lucia in 1994, more than 60% of the island's crop was lost. Banana farmers recovered only to face a more permanent and damaging setback. In 1995, a ruling by the World Trade Organization (WTO) eliminated the British system of price subsidies and protected access to the European market that favoured producers in the former Windward colonies. The WTO legislation has resulted in falling prices and hard times for most small farmers already burdened by high labour and transportation costs.

In addition to bananas, the island also produces coconuts, vegetables, citrus fruits, root crops and cocoa. In St. Lucia, agriculture is an important part of the economy because it provides income to a broad section of the population. Agriculture employs 43% of the workforce, and of that number 83% are small farmers who own less than 2ha (5 acres) of land. For many low income families, subsistence farming is their only means of survival.

Like most Caribbean nations, tourism has taken over as the most important foreign exchange earner for St. Lucia. Unfortunately, a clear lack of planning characterized early tourism ventures in the 1960s and 70s but the situation has changed dramatically since then. Now government efforts to broaden the benefits of tourism and a determination to promote the island's abundant natural attractions are going a long way towards making tourism a sustainable economic option.

Today, the island's greatest challenge is to expand its small manufacturing sector—not an easy task for an island with a small population and few natural resources. But the more diversified St. Lucia's economy can become, the less vulnerable it will be to market fluctuations. Although there are factories involved in garment making, handicrafts, beverages, electronic assembly and coconut oil, the country remains heavily dependent on imports, mainly from the U.K. The latest period of economic growth, particularly in the tourism industry, has put even greater pressure on the economy to generate enough foreign exchange revenue to pay for expensive imported goods, like cars and mechanical equipment.

St. Lucia is also struggling with chronic unemployment, at about 25%. The persistant lack of job opportunities on the smaller islands of the Caribbean has made economic migration to England or North America a necessity for many Lucians.

Population

Over 90% of St. Lucia's 156,000 citizens are of African descent. The balance of the population is predominantly of East Indian origin with a tiny European community. While the Africans arrived as slaves, most East Indians are descendants of indentured labourers brought to the Caribbean by the British government in the 19th and early 20th century. With the end of slavery, they provided an alternative source of cheap labour for plantation owners seeking to delay the decline of the sugar industry on several islands. After a five-year term as field-hands in exchange for free passage, room and board, they were given land or cash and the choice of returning to India or a new life in the Caribbean.

English, the official language, is spoken by everyone on the island. St. Lucia, along with Dominica, Martinique and Haiti, is also a member of Bannzil Kwéyòl, the International Organization of Creole Speaking Countries. Traditionally an oral language, Creole, or patois ("patwa") as it is commonly referred to by Lucians, has been used on the island for hundreds of years. The slaves who came to the West Indies were taken from many different parts of Africa, each with its own unique customs and languages. Patois was an ingenious means of overcoming these language barriers without being easily understood by the European masters. Similar to that spoken in Martinique, Lucian patois is a simplified but vaguely recognizable mix of French vocabulary, African syntax and some English terms and phrases that have recently entered the language.

In the midst of a trend toward Americanization in Lucian society, patois usage has declined, particularly among the youth. It remains, however, a fundamental part of rural culture and a necessary feature of any politician's speech. Recently, the government has taken measures to preserve and celebrate Creole culture (see below).

St. Lucia's population is 90% Roman Catholic, a legacy of distant colonial ties with France. The first Catholic church was built in Soufrière in 1746 and its influence quickly grew to include the control of many schools and hospitals. There are also a small number of Anglican parishes but the fastest-growing religious organization on the island is the Seventh Day Adventists. The large tents you may see around the island are set up for their revival meetings.

Arts and Culture

Festivals

St. Lucia's folk culture is celebrated annually in several colourful, often boisterous, festivals. The **Jounen Kwéyòl Festival** was recently conceived to promote the island's Creole heritage. The final day of festivities on October 28 culminates a month of cultural activities and competitions held throughout the island. The event starts early. In the crowd are young women dressed in the *wob dwiyel*, traditional Creole skirts and *tête-en-l'air* headpieces; *boisbois* men on stilts, skillfully making their way through the party on the street; and on centre stage, couples gracefully dancing the *vyolon* and the *kwadil* to the music of a Creole band. Celebrations take place in several different communities, each on its own scale, with its own style. A visit to any one of them is not only entertaining and enjoyable, but a first-rate cultural experience.

St. Lucia's two oldest cultural institutions are the societies of **La Rose** and **La Marguerite**. As early as 1769, slaves organized these secret societies, both as support networks and as forums for disguised political expression. Living in the midst of slavery and constant battles between the French and English for possession of the island, each society identified itself with one of the colonial powers: La Marguerite with the English and La Rose the French. Herein lies the source of the playful antagonisms between the two societies. Over the past 200 years, each group has developed its own styles and protocol.

La Marguerite, for example, tends to take a formalized approach to its rituals and songs while La Rose's performances and gatherings are more emotive and impromptu in nature.

The societies are organized in the form of a mock kingdom. Members elect a king and queen to represent them along with a coterie of princes, princesses, magistrates and even policemen. Everyone dresses the part with much good humour. The heart of the society is its *chantwel*, a singer of traditional songs, who performs at all the group's meetings, called *seeances*. *Belairs,* or traditional songs, are a source of rivalry between the two groups. Typically, they praise the *chantwel's* group or poke fun at the other society. La Rose *chantwels* are usually accompanied by traditional percussion instruments like the *tanbouwen* (tambourine), the *baha* (a long tube with fingerholes) and a *chakchak* (rattle). A La Marguerite *chantwel*, on the other hand, will tend to use a guitar, *quatro* (banjo) and violin.

The best time to experience the fun and ceremony of these societies is during the festival days, when they honour their patron Saints, Marguerite Marie and Rose de Lima. Grand fetes with singing, dancing and "royal elections" are held for La Marguerite on October 17 and for La Rose on August 30.

Popularized in Trinidad, Carnival is St. Lucia's most popular and exciting festival. It is one of the few events that involves every layer of Lucian society regardless of class. The festival's sensual atmosphere is rooted in its connection with pre-Lenten celebrations. The term "carnival" is a combination of *carne* or flesh and *vale* or farewell. In other words, this is a time to enjoy physical pleasures before Lent's abstinence.

In its earliest manifestations, carnival was associated with plantation life and *canboulay,* meaning burning of the cane. After the sugar harvest, when cane fields were burned, slaves celebrated the end of a long period of hard work with African-style drumming, dances, and costumes. Eventually, some plantation owners joined the festivities wearing slave costumes, prompting slaves to don costumes imitating their masters. It wasn't until the end of slavery, when blacks integrated *canboulay* street processions with their freedom marches in the cities that it be-

came associated with the coming of Lent. Before emancipation, the pre-Lenten celebrations of church mass and costume parties were almost exclusively white Creole affairs. Gradually, the two traditions merged and by 1947 Lucians celebrated their first official carnival.

Today, carnival features the glitter and imagination of the costume competitions, steel bands, soca music, parades, street parties and calypso singers. It usually takes place in February or March.

Music

Lucians take their music very seriously. The highly successful **St. Lucia Jazz Festival** takes place in May and the **Country Music Festival** in December. From car stereos and house speakers you'll hear reggae, soca, and even country and western music. None, however, is as popular as calypso, which arouses the passion of the nation. Developed to a fine art in Trinidad, good calypso involves both spirited performance and inspired lyrics. It centres around one singer, a calypsonian, and the skill with which he or she uses lyrics to comment on current social and political issues or chastise prominent people in Lucian society.

Visual Arts

For such a small nation, St. Lucia has produced many distinguished artists. **Llewellyn Xavier** is an internationally acclaimed multimedia artist and painter who has exhibited in Italy, England, Canada, and the United States. Much of his work explores the natural world and environmental themes. **Dunstan St. Omer**, a painter and teacher, is best known for a series of church murals entitled the *Black Madonna* that decorate altars in Monchy, Martinique and Trinidad. In the Caribbean of the early 1970s, his Afrocentric interpretation of Christianity was revolutionary in that it expressed a new consciousness not only among Lucians, but all Caribbean peoples. To experience a younger generation of Lucian artists like Donna Gomez, Arnold Toulon or Daniel-Jean Baptiste, there are private or artist-run galleries in each of the island's major centres.

Literature

In the literary world, **Derek Walcott** stands alone in the height of his achievements. Winner of the 1992 Nobel Prize for literature, Walcott is a distinguished poet, playwright and teacher. Books such as *In a Green Night*, *The Castaway* and *The Fortunate Traveller* are considered classics and have influenced writers across the Caribbean and worldwide. **Garth St. Omer** is another prominent Lucian writer. A novelist, he has also taught literature in the United States and Ghana. Two of his most famous works are *A Room on the Hill* and *Shades of Gray*.

Architecture

In cities and villages around St. Lucia, many wonderful examples of traditional Caribbean architecture still exist. The real beauty of traditional Lucian architecture is how it exemplifies both the creative flair and ingenuity of the Caribbean people. Each element in the design, including the elaborate ornamentation, is an adaptation to the region's climatic extremes of heat, rain and hurricanes. A large verandah provides a comfortable social space and keeps a house's interior temperature down by keeping direct sunlight off the main walls. The fanciful wood trim along a roof or porch is picturesque but it also diffuses the sun's rays.

Dormer windows are a common feature of many old homes in St. Lucia. At one time, blocks of ice would be placed at these windows to cool off the air flow into the upper floor.

During the rainy season, a steep gabled roof drains the water away. In the middle of a hurricane, gables expose less surface area to high winds than flat roofs, minimizing the possibility of a suction force tearing off the roof. Moreover, a thick stone wall and foundation keep a house intact in spite of severe storms and floods.

Nowadays, traditional architecture is unfortunately less prevalent than a concrete block style of modern construction which is cheaper and in some ways stronger, but aesthetically hideous. The threat of fire is also a major concern, especially for many Lucians who remember how fires wiped out large sections of Castries and Soufrière. The older wooden plank homes, so common a few decades ago, were particularly vulnerable to such tragedy. Most were built using cuts of pine timber known as sap wood. Though it is an exceptionally strong and durable building aterial, pine sap also happens to be an extremely flammable substance.

Typical Creole country house

Practical Information

The following chapter provides information that will help you prepare for your trip to St. Lucia and make the most of your stay once you arrive.

Entrance Formalities

Passport and Visa

A passport is not required for citizens of Canada, the United States, the United Kingdom or Commonwealth countries. A birth certificate or proof of citizenship will suffice. Bringing a passport, however, is strongly recommended. Nationals of other countries must apply for a visa from a St. Lucia consulate in their home country (see p 49). A normal tourist visa is valid for 42 days. Every visitor must have an onward ticket. No vaccination certificates are required unless you are arriving from an infected country.

Visa Extensions

A 21-day visa extension costs $40 EC and is avail-

able to all nationals. You must present a passport or national identification card with proof of an onward ticket. Both must still be valid after the extension expires. Applications are submitted in person at the Immigration office at Police Headquarters on Bridge

Street by Castries River in Castries. The length of time it takes to process your application depends on your nationality. If you arrive early in the morning, it's possible to have it done the same day; otherwise, you can wait up to three days.

Customs

Tourists may bring in 200 cigarettes or 250g (8.75oz) of tobacco and one litre (40oz) of liquor or wine.

Departure Tax

The departure tax for all nationals leaving by air is $21 US or $54 EC. Credit cards are not accepted. The fee is paid at your airline's ticket counter.

Embassies and Consulates

Foreign Embassies and Consulates in St. Lucia

There are no Australian, Canadian or U.S. embassies in St. Lucia. The nearest ones, located in Barbados, are listed below.

Australian High Commission
Bishop's Court Hill, St. Michael
Bridgetown, Barbados
☎(246) 435-2834

British High Commission
NIS Building, 24 Micoud St.,
Second Floor
Castries, St. Lucia
☎(452) 2484 or 2485 or 2486
≈(452) 453-1543

Canadian High Commission
Bishop's Court Hill,
P.O. Box 404, St. Michael
Bridgetown, Barbados
☎(246) 429-3550
≈(246) 429-3780

French Embassy
Clarke Ave.,
Vigie, St. Lucia
☎452-2462 or 452-5877
≈452-7899

Honorary Consul for the Federal Republic of Germany
P.O. Box 2023,
Gros Islet, St. Lucia
☎450-8050
≈450-0255

Italian Vice Consulate
Reduit, P.O. Box GM 848,
Castries, St. Lucia
☎452-0865 or 452-0866
≈452-0869
casalucia@candw.lc

Netherlands Consulate
M&C Building, Bridge St.,
P.O. Box 1020,
Castries, St. Lucia
☎452-2811
≈452-3592

Norwegian Consulate
Barnard Sons Building, Bridge St.,
P.O. Box 169,
Castries, St. Lucia
☎*452-2216*
⇄*453-1394*

U.S. Embassy
P.O. Box 302
Bridgetown, Barbados
West Indies
☎*(246) 431-0225*
⇄*(246) 431-0179*

St. Lucia's Embassies and Consulates Abroad

CANADA
(For Ontario, Alberta, British Columbia, Manitoba, Saskatchewan)
Consulate General of St. Lucia
8 King St. E., suite 700-701
Toronto, ON M5C 1B5
☎*(416) 203-8400*
⇄*(416) 203-8486*
sluconca@ionsys.com

(For Ottawa and other provinces)
Organization of Eastern Caribbean States High Commission
130 Albert St., suite 700
Ottawa, ON K1P 5G4
☎*(613) 236-8952*

EUROPEAN UNION
East Caribbean States Mission to the European Union
Rue de Livorne 42, B-1050,
Brussels, Belgium
☎*(011) 322-534-2611*
⇄*(011) 322-539-4009*
www.caribisles.org

United Kingdom
High Commission for St. Lucia
10 Kensington Court,
London, England W8 5DL
☎*(011)-44-71-937-9522*
⇄*(011)-44-71-937-8704*

UNITED STATES

New York
St. Lucia Consulate-General
800 Second Ave., 9th floor
New York, NY 10017
☎*(212) 697-9360*
⇄*(212) 697-4993*
slumission@aol.com

Washington
Embassy of St. Lucia
3216 New Mexico Ave., NW
Washington, DC 20016
☎*(202) 364-6792*
⇄*(202) 364-6723*

Practical Information

Tourist Information

St. Lucia Tourism Offices Abroad

CANADA
8 King St. E., suite 700
Toronto, ON M5C 1B5
☎*(416) 362-4242*
⇄*(416) 362-7832*

FRANCE
53 Rue Francois Ler
Paris 75008
☎*47-20-39-66*
⇄*47-23-09-65*

St. Lucia on the Internet

St. Lucia Tourist Board
www.interknowledge.com/st-lucia
www.candw.lc/stlucia.htm

St. Lucia Hotel and Tourism Association
www.stluciatravel.com.lc

Travel Information
www.sluonestop.com
www.stluciatravel.com

St. Lucia – Country Profile
www.cananews.com/cbi/profilestlucia.htm

St. Lucia Jazz Festival
http://stluciajazz.com

Guided Tour – St. Lucia
www.mygale.org/04/schmittg/index_a.html

Great Links
www.lucianstuff.i.am

Government Information Service
www.stlucia.gov.lc/gis

Funky Creole Cooking
www.cookingwithkouly.com

Creole Culture
www.saint-lucia.blackorama.com
www.stluciatravel.com.lc
www.siu.edu/departments/cola/ling/reports/stlucian/de
script.htm
www.sil.org/ethnologue/countries/stLu.htm

Photographs
www.golden.net/~chiggins
www.galen.u-max.com/stlucia.htm

GERMANY
P.O. Box 1525
61366 Friedrichsdorf
☎*011-49-6172-778013*
⇌*011-49-6172-778033*
st.luciads@t-online.de

UNITED KINGDOM
421a Finchley Rd.
London, NW3 6HJ
☎*01-44-171-431-3675*
⇌*01-44-171-431-7920*
st.lucia@pwaxis.com.uk

Tourism Information on the Island

Official tourist information offices are located in all major centres on the island. In the north and east, hotel staff can answer any questions.

Vieux Fort

every day noon to last flight
Hewanorra Airport
☎*454-6644*

Castries

Point Seraphine Duty-Free Complex
Mon-Fri 9am to 5pm, Sat 9am to 2pm and, if a cruise ship is in port, Sun 9am to 4pm
P.O. Box 221, Castries
☎*452-4094 or 452-5968*
⇌*453-1121*

Vigie Airport
every day noon to last flight
☎*452-2596*

Downtown Castries
*Mon-Fri 8am to 4pm;
Sat 9am to 1pm*
Jeremie St.
☎*452-2479*

Soufrière
*Mon-Fri 8am to noon and
1pm to 4pm; Sat 8am to noon*
Bay St.
☎*459-7419*

Magazine Articles

Outpost
"St. Lucia: An Island Apart"
March/April 2000
by Chris Higgins

National Geographic Traveler
"St. Lucia: Winter Escape to an Easygoing Island"
January/February 1996
by Bryan Di Salvatore

Getting There

By Plane

St. Lucia is serviced by several international and regional airlines. Most offer reasonable one- or two-week charter packages. For longer stays, fares tend to be a bit expensive, depending on the season you travel. In some cases, it may even be cheaper to buy two charter fares rather than paying the full fare.

Liat Airlines, a regional carrier, offers several great

packages for island hopping. Their Explorer pass allows you to travel to three islands for $262 US or from three to six islands for only $85 US each. The passes can be purchased from your local travel agent or from Liat representatives in the Caribbean.

The following airlines offer direct flights to St. Lucia:

Air Canada
50 Micoud St.
Castries
☎*451-6406 or 452-6481*
⇌*451-6408*

Air France
Bridge St.
Castries
☎*458-8282 or 458-8283*
⇌*458-8259*

Air Jamaica
36 Micoud St.
Castries
☎*453-6611*
⇌*459-0592*

American Airlines
50 Micoud St.
Castries
☎*454-6777 or 454-6795*
⇌*453-6358*

British Airways
William Peter Blvd.
Castries
☎*452-3951 or 452-7444*
⇌*452-2900*

BWIA International
22 Micoud St.
Castries
☎*452-3778 or 452-3789*
⇌*452-2054*

Airports

Hewanorra International Airport
Vieux Fort
☎*454-6355 or 454-6782*
Car rentals, tourist information, foreign exchange, restaurant and duty-free shopping are available.

George F. L. Charles Airport
Vigie
☎*452-1156*
This mainly regional airport has car rentals, currency exchange and tourist information available. Taxis can transport you to your hotel. A less expensive alternative is to walk the length of the runway to the main road. From there, you can get a local minibus into Castries or to the north for less than $2 EC.

By Boat

St. Lucia is a popular stop for cruise ships. From sailing adventures on authentic sailboats to luxurious cruise liners, there are a number of options available depending on your budget and taste.

One of the best ways to experience the Caribbean is

by inter-island ferry. Two companies operate passenger and cargo services in the Eastern Caribbean. **Windward Lines** sails to St. Lucia, Barbados, St. Vincent, Trinidad and Venezuela. The sleeping facilities are excellent and food is served on board. **L'Express des Iles** operates a passenger and car ferry to Guadeloupe, Dominica and Martinique, as well as to St. Lucia. Both have great package deals available for island hopping. All passenger ships coming to St. Lucia dock in Castries.

Windward Lines
c/o Mendes Shipping
Valco Building, Cadet St., Castries
☎*452-1364*
≈*453-1654*
www.infinetworx.com/windward

L'Express des Iles
c/o Cox and Company Ltd.
Wm. Peter Blvd., Castries
☎*452-2211*
≈*453-1868*
www.express-des-iles.com

If you're sailing your own boat, Rodney Bay's world class marina facilities include telecommunication and banking services, boat repair, restaurants and a well-stocked grocery store. There are also picturesque anchor sites all along the island's Caribbean coast.

Finding Your Way Around

St. Lucia is divided into 11 administrative districts called quarters. This can be slightly confusing since each of them is also named after a major town in the district. For example, there is the Quarter of Gros Islet as well as the town of Gros Islet or the Quarter of Castries and the city of Castries. To avoid confusion, assume the place-names in this guide refer to the town unless otherwise specified.

Distances are short in St. Lucia so getting around the island is easy, whatever your budget.

By Plane

Chartering a helicopter or airplane will get you across the island in minutes. Bookings can be made at both airports (see p 52). They are, however, expensive so unless you're pressed for time or just want to take in the spectacular aerial scenery, you don't need to spend the money.

Helenair
☎*452-7196 or 7112 or 452-1958*

Paradise Helicopters
☎*450-9203*
≈*450-9205*

Practical
Information

St. Lucia Helicopters
☎ *453-6950*
 452-1553

By Bus

For the majority of Lucians, minibuses are the primary method of public transport. For travellers, they are a convenient, safe and economical way of getting around the island. The music is good too! Public minibuses are owned by private operators and usually identifiable by an *H* in the front windshield. They leave from terminals only when they are full. All you have to do is stand by the road (heading in your direction) and when one comes along wave your hand down toward the ground. When you want to get off, just tell the driver.

Bus Routes Around the Island

Castries–Gros Islet
(drivers do not normally go north of Gros Islet unless paid extra)

Castries–Soufriere

Soufriere–Vieux Fort

Vieux Fort–Micoud–Dennery–Castries

Buses run in both directions. Other routes exist to connect interior communities with the main highway.

By Boat

Unfortunately, there is no public ferry system operating on the island. In Castries and Rodney Bay, however, there are ferries with routes covering the local vicinity. You can charter a water taxi to go anywhere you want on the island. Half- or full-day tours can also be booked to certain attractions. Hiring a boat on your own is an expensive proposition but, for groups of four, rates are actually quite reasonable, considering the beautiful coastal scenery and warm seabreeze. Sailboat charters are also available.

Several companies offer half- and full-day cruises. The tour groups can be rather large but the full-day tour includes snorkelling and visits to some of the island's most popular attractions.

By Car

Renting a vehicle gives you the freedom to explore remote areas and create your own itinerary. Gasoline is reasonably priced and stations are located all over the island. Unfortunately, however, the profusion of cars on the island is beginning to have an environmental impact. If you plan on visiting the more inaccessible areas, especially along the east coast, a four-wheel-drive vehicle is essential. Otherwise, a more affordable compact car will be fine. Road maps are free at hotels and tourism offices. A more detailed road map (1:50,000) is available at the Department of Survey and Mapping in Castries for $20 EC *(1st fl., Graham Louisy Building, John Compton Hwy.,* ☎*468-4468)* For planning your own road trip, it is an indispensable tool.

Car Rental Requirements

In order to rent a car, the driver must be 25 years of age or older and have at least three years of driving experience. A local driving permit is required which can easily be obtained from your car rental agency. The standard fee is $20 US or $54 EC. Every company also requires either a cash deposit or a signed credit card slip. Curiously, a Collision Damage Waiver is optional. It is strongly recommended you sign on for the insurance package. Not signing means you're completely liable for expenses incurred in the event of an accident.

Car Rental Companies

Cool Breeze
☎*459-7729*
⇌*459-5309*

Courtesy Car Rentals
☎*452-8140*
⇌*452-9566*

CTL Rent a Car
☎*452-0732 or 452-0932*
⇌*458-0660*

Progressive Car Rental
☎/⇌*450-2733*

St. Lucia National Car Services Ltd.
☎*450-8500*
⇌*450-8577*

Scooters

Rodeo Rentals
☎*452-0189*
⇌*458-0078*

Motorcycles

Wayne's Motorcycle Centre
☎/⇌*452-2059*

Driving Precautions

First and foremost, drive on the *left*-hand side of the road. For North Americans, this can be disorienting at first. Take your time and warm up before driving in Castries. While driving in the mountainous regions be aware of the deep rain gutters at the edge of the roadway.

In St. Lucia, as in much of the Caribbean, the car horn is a tool for communication. Among other things, drivers use it to say hello or to warn oncoming traffic as they round the bend of a sharp curve. In the steep mountains of the south, this practice is strongly recommended. Remember to slow down in village areas and watch for children. Lastly, please do not drive on the beaches to avoid disturbing the turtles who breed there.

By Taxi

Taxis are a good idea if you prefer to sit back, relax and enjoy your ride around the island. For travellers on a budget, however, they can be expensive. But this option provides privacy and the drivers are informative and friendly. Normally, drivers offer half- and full-day fixed-rate packages to visit attractions around the island. A list of local taxi operators can be obtained from your hotel desk or tourist board offices.

Hitchhiking

Hitchhiking is a common practice around the island, particularly in rural areas. Outside major centres, you can try it anywhere. A wave of the hand towards the ground is the proper gesture. Although hitchhiking is a great way to get to know the local people, there are risks, especially for women travelling alone. That applies in any country, including St. Lucia. Travellers will find minibuses are so frequent and cheap here that hitchhiking is not really necessary.

Money and Banking

Currency

St. Lucia's currency is the Eastern Caribbean dollar. Merchants will also accept US cash. 100 cents = 1 EC Dollar

All the prices in this guidebook are listed in EC dollars unless otherwise indicated.

Foreign Exchange

Exchanging currency in St. Lucia is easy. All the banks and major hotels have foreign exchange counters. Services are also available at Pointe Seraphine duty-free mall in Vigie and the duty-free shopping complex in Castries and at both airports. The normal rate is approximately $2.70 EC to $1 US, or slightly less at hotels or stores (see p 57).

Exchange Rates*

$1 EC	=	$0.57 CAN	1$ CAN	=	$1.76 EC
$1 EC	=	$0.37 US	1$ US	=	$2.67 EC
$1 EC	=	£0.27	£1	=	$3.71 EC
$1 EC	=	0.67 SF	1 SF	=	$1.49 EC
$1 EC	=	0.44 € (euro)	1 € (euro) =		$2.28 EC
$1 EC	=	2.88 FF	1 FF	=	$0.35 EC
$1 EC	=	0.86 DM	1 DM	=	$1.16 EC
$1 EC	=	0.97 DG	1 DG	=	$1.03 EC

*Samples only—rates fluctuate

Banks and ATMs

A large number of foreign and domestic banks operate around the island. They can assist you with money transfers, currency exchange and credit card advances. Banks are closed weekends and holidays with the exception of Saturday mornings for branches at the Rodney Bay marina. Normal hours are Monday to Thursday 8am to 3pm and Friday 8am to 5pm. To avoid lineups, arrive early in the morning. If you're travelling in rural areas, bring enough US or EC cash for the duration of your stay and include some smaller denominations for minor transactions.

In the cities, automated teller machines (ATMs) are common and the quickest way to get money. They all accept Mastercard or Visa for cash advances and most are linked to the Cirrus, Interac or PLUS systems for account withdrawals. They only dispense funds in EC currency.

Barclays Bank
Castries
☎456-1000

Royal Bank of Canada
Castries
☎452-2245

National Commercial Bank of St. Lucia
Castries
☎456-6000

Credit Cards

Visa, MasterCard, American Express and, to a lesser extent, Diners Club are accepted by merchants, restaurants and hotels.

Traveller's Cheques

In St. Lucia, banks, hotels and even some merchants can cash traveller's cheques. You will need a passport or a national identity card. American Express has an office in Castries (*20 Micoud St.,* ☎ *452-1529*). Be sure to record your serial numbers separately (give this to someone at home) so they can be cancelled or replaced if they are lost or stolen. Although traveller's cheques are the safest way to travel with money, it's also a good idea to bring a supply of US cash for emergencies, weekends and to take advantage of merchant discounts.

Language

English is the official language and is spoken everywhere. Patois or Creole is still common, especially in rural areas.

Climate

St. Lucia is hot all year round. Daily temperatures are normally about 26°C (80°F). The hottest time of year is from June to August. The tropical heat also makes it humid. Fortunately, the trade winds provide a constant cool breeze that gives some relief from the heat.

The rainy season is from June to November. The wettest areas are the southern mountains and in the rain forest. The term "rainy season" is a bit misleading, however. During this time, showers are brief—prolonged downpours are rare. It is certainly cloudier but that helps diffuse the intense Caribbean sun. Temperatures are still very warm and sunny most of the day. The driest and sunniest periods, however, are February and March.

The only major concern when planning a trip to St. Lucia is the hurricane season between June and November. At this time there is also the potential risk of confronting a powerful tropical storm or cyclone.

Health

St. Lucia is a wonderful country to explore and boasts top-rate medical facilities. You do not need any vaccinations to enter St. Lucia, unless you have recently visited an area where yellow fever is common.

Cases of illnesses like Hepatitis B, AIDS and certain venereal diseases have been reported; it is therefore a good idea to be careful. Condoms are the best protection against these illnesses.

Remember that consuming too much alcohol, particularly during prolonged exposure to the sun, can cause severe dehydration and lead to health problems.

If you get a case of diarrhea, soothe your stomach by avoiding solids; instead, drink carbonated beverages, bottled water, or weak tea (avoid milk) until you recover. As dehydration can be dangerous, drinking sufficient quantities of liquid is crucial. Pharmacies sell various preparations to treat diarrhea, with different effects. Pepto Bismol and Imodium will stop the diarrhea which slows the loss of fluids. They should be avoided, however, if you have a fever since they will prevent the necessary elimination of bacteria. Oral rehydration products such as Gastrolyte will replace the minerals and electrolytes that your body has lost as a result of the diarrhea. In a pinch, you can make your own rehydration solution by mixing one litre of pure water with one teaspoon of sugar and two or three teaspoons of salt. After the diarrhea has subsided, eat easily digested foods like rice to give your stomach time to adjust. If symptoms become more serious (high fever, persistent diarrhea), see a doctor as antibiotics may be necessary.

Nutrition and climate can also cause problems. Pay attention to food freshness and the cleanliness of the preparation area. Good hygiene (wash your hands often) will help avoid undesirable situations.

Water

All the tap water in St. Lucia is safe to drink. If you prefer to drink bottled water, however, it is sold everywhere.

Insects

A nuisance common to many countries, bugs can be a big problem in St. Lucia, particularly mosquitoes and sand flies. Mosquitoes are generally more numerous in the summer, when there is more rain and at nightfall. Sand flies, also called "no-see-'ems" by locals because they are so small (they can even get through screens), are perhaps the most annoying. They also come out at nightfall and are particularly prevalent near windless beaches on the lee side of an island. Their bite does not so much itch as burn.

The best way to deal with these two critters is with a good insect repellent. Repellents with DEET are the most effective. The concentration of DEET varies from one product to the next; the higher the concentration, the longer the protection. A concentration of 35% DEET will protect for 4 to 6hrs, while 95% will last from 10 to 12hrs. New formulas with DEET are available in lesser concentrations, but last just as long.

To further reduce the possibility of getting bitten, do not wear perfume or bright colours. Sundown is an especially active time for insects. When walking in wooded areas, cover your legs and ankles well. Insect coils can help provide a better night's sleep. Before bed, apply insect repellent to your skin and to the headboard and baseboard of your bed. If possible, get an air-conditioned room, or bring a mosquito net.

Lastly, since it is impossible to completely avoid contact with mosquitoes, bring along a cream to soothe the bites you will invariably get.

And try not to scratch—scratching a bite will only activate the allergen and make things worse. A bite that is left alone will go away much faster.

Plants

A concern in beach areas is the **manchineel tree**. It is identifiable by its green leaves, yellow stems and apple-like green fruit. A closer look reveals a tiny dot where leaf meets leaf stalk. Contact with sap from the leaves and bark brings on blisters and a very uncomfortable stinging sensation. The fruit is also poisonous. The best way to avoid problems is by simply staying away from the tree, especially while it is raining, as sap will drip down from the branches. If you do come in contact with the sap, wash it off your skin with water immediately to prevent a blister.

Animals

The only animal that can be considered dangerous to humans in St. Lucia is the **St. Lucian viper** or **fer de lance** (see p 16). This light brown snake prefers grassy areas like those along the southeast coast. You are unlikely to ever see one, but to be safe, avoid putting your hands into holes or crevices and do not step off the trail in tall grass. Bites are very rare but extremely dangerous and require immediate medical attention.

The Sun

While the sun brings many benefits, it also brings its share of ill effects. Always wear sunscreen. Many creams on the market do not offer adequate protection; ask a pharmacist. Too much sun can cause sunstroke (dizziness, vomiting, fever). Be careful, especially the first few days after arriving, as it takes time to get used to the sun. Take sun in small doses and protect yourself with a hat and sunglasses. Many people don't realize the risk of sunburn while snorkeling—a good waterproof sunscreen is imperative.

Jet Lag and Motion Sickness

The discomfort of jet lag is inevitable. Some tricks might help lessen it, but remember that the best way to get through it is to give your body time to adapt. You can even start adjusting to your new time gradually before your departure and on the airplane. Eat well and drink a lot of water. You are strongly advised to force yourself to switch to the new time as soon as you arrive. Stay awake if is morning and go to sleep if it is evening. This way your body will become adjusted more quickly.

To minimize the discomfort of motion sickness, avoid the jolts as much as possible and keep your eyes on the horizon (for example, sit in the middle of a boat or in the front of a car or a bus). Eat small, light meals, both before leaving and during the journey. There are accessories and medications that can help reduce symptoms such as nausea. Some friendly advice: try to relax and think about something else!

Practical Information

First-Aid Kit

A small first-aid kit can prove useful, and should be carefully prepared before leaving home. Bring along sufficient amounts of any medications you take regularly, as well as a valid prescription. Also bring along the prescription for your glasses or contact lenses. Your kit should also include:

- adhesive bandages
- a disinfectant
- an analgesic
- antihistamines
- tablets for upset stomach or motion sickness

Don't forget to include your contact lens solution, and an extra pair of glasses, if applicable.

Insurance

Health

Health insurance is the most important type of insurance for travellers. A comprehensive health insurance policy that provides sufficient coverage to pay for hospitalization, nursing care and doctor's fees is recommended. Keep in mind that health care costs are rising quickly everywhere. The policy should also have a repatriation clause in case the required care is not available in St. Lucia. As patients are sometimes asked to pay for medical services up front, find out what provisions your policy makes in this event. Always carry your health insurance policy with you when travelling to avoid problems if you are in an accident, and get receipts for any expenses incurred.

Theft

Most residential insurance policies cover a percentage of personal belongings against theft if the items are stolen outside the country. If you plan on travelling with valuable objects, check your policy or with an insurance agency to see whether additional baggage insurance is necessary. To file an insurance claim for a theft incurred while on holiday, you will need a police report from the country you are visiting.

Cancellation

This type of insurance is usually offered by your travel agent when you purchase your air tickets or tour package. It covers any non-refundable payments to travel suppliers such as airlines, and it must be purchased at the same time as initial payment is made for air tickets or tour packages. Trip cancellation insurance comes into effect if a traveller has to call off a trip for valid medical reasons or because of a death in the family. This type of insurance can be useful, but weigh the likelihood of your using it against the price. It is a good idea when booking into smaller resorts where deposits can be required two months in advance.

Mail and Telecommunications

Mail

There is a post office in every town and city. Normally, they are open Monday to Friday, 8:15am to 4:30pm, but that can vary somewhat from region to region. The postal service is dependable and reasonably priced. There is no zip code system in St. Lucia.

Post Restante services are offered at each branch. Have mail sent to you c/o Post Restante with your given name first and surname highlighted. In Castries, the Post Restante counter is at the General Post Office. You will find it by looking outside, around the corner of the main entrance, by the National Development Building.

Telecommunications

The country code for St. Lucia is **758**. There are no area codes on the island. Dial "0" for the operator and "411" for directory assistance. Cable and Wireless is the national phone company. Generally, it's not difficult to find a public phone in St. Lucia and you can easily make calls from your hotel. Phone cards can be purchased at Cable and Wireless outlets or shops in denominations of $10 EC, $20 EC, $40 EC and $20 US. Long-distance calls can also be made with your credit card by dialling 811.

Direct Dialling

USA and Canada: dial 1 + area code + number

Other countries: dial 011 + country code + number

UK: dial 011 + 44 + area code + number

Country Codes:
Australia **61**
Belgium **32**
Denmark **45**
France **33**
Germany **49**
Italy **39**
Netherlands **31**
Norway **47**
Sweden **46**

Collect calls are very costly. A more economical option is to use one of the Direct Phone services.

USA Direct
☎*800-872-2881*

Call USA
☎*800-674-7000*

Practical Information

Canada Direct
800-744-2580

British Telecom Direct Service
800-342-5284

Internet Services

Cable and Wireless operates three e-mail service centres:

Castries
Bridge St.
☎*453-9000*

Choc Bay
Gablewoods Mall N.
☎*453-9900*

Vieux Fort
JQ's Plaza
☎*453-9900*

Some merchants have also set up Internet services:

The Internet Cafe
Rodney Bay
☎*452-0932*
ctlslu@candw.lc

Pegasus Tours and Internet
☎*458-3049*
pegasustours@candw.lc

PC Tech Plus
Castries
☎*453-6526*
pceaglestar@hotmail.com

Business Hours and Holidays

Opening hours for stores are Monday to Saturday from 9am to 5pm. Restaurants and businesses involved with tourism are usually open Sundays.

Holidays

New Year's
January 1-2

Independence Day
February 22

Good Friday
April (varies)

Easter Monday
April (varies)

Labour Day
May 1

Whit Monday
June 12

Corpus Christi
June 22

Emancipation Day
August 7

Thanksgiving Day
October 2

National Day
December 13

Christmas Day
December 25

Boxing Day
December 26

Festivals

St. Lucia Jazz Festival
May 5 -14

Petit Piton, a volcanic rock formation that soars 750m (2,461ft) high, is an irresistible challenge for ardent hikers. Ample reward awaits for them on their way down.... - *Chris Higgins*

This farmer's shelter in Fond St. Jacques looks like it's in danger of being reclaimed by the surrounding forest.- *Chris Higgins*

Feast of St. Rose de Lima
August 30

Feast of La Marguerite
October 17

**Jounen Kwéyòl Entenasiyonnal
(International Creole Day)**
October 29

All Saints day
November 1

All Souls Day
November 2

St. Cecilia's Day (feast of musicians)
November 22

Atlantic Rally Crossing
November 23

Festival of Lights and Renewal
December 13

Identity and Culture Shock

Before going on vacation, we pack our luggage and get the necessary vaccinations and travel documents, but rarely do we prepare for culture shock. The following text explains what culture shock is and how to deal with it.

In a nutshell, culture shock can be defined as a certain anxiety that may be experienced upon arriving in another country where everything is different, including the culture and language, making communication as you know it very difficult. Combined with jetlag and fatigue, the strain of orienting yourself in a new cultural context can lead to psychological stress that may throw you off track.

Culture shock is a frustrating phenomenon that can easily turn travellers setting out with the best of intentions into intolerant, racist and ethnocentric ones—they may come to believe that their society is better than the new, and seemingly incomprehensible, one. This type of reaction detracts from the whole travel experience.

People in other countries have different customs and lifestyles that are sometimes hard for us to understand or accept. We might even find ourselves wondering how people can live the way they do when their customs run contrary to what we deem to be "normal." In the end, however, it is easier to adapt to them than to criticize or disregard them.

Even though this is the era of globalization and cultural homogenization, we still live in a world of many "worlds," such as the business world, the worlds of different continents, suburbia, and the world of the rich and the poor. Of course, these worlds intersect, but each has its own

Practical
Information

characteristic set of ideas and cultural values. Furthermore, even if they are not in direct contact, each has at least an image of the other (which is often distorted and nothing more). And if a picture is worth a thousand words, then our world contains million upon millions of them. Sometimes it is hard to tell what is real and what isn't, but one thing is certain: what you see on television about a place is not the same as when you get there.

When people interact with each other, they inevitably make sense of each other through their differences. The strength of a group, human or animal, lies in its diversity, whether it be in genetics or ideas. Can you imagine how boring the world would be if everyone were the same?

Travelling can be seen as a way of developing a more holistic, or global, vision of the world; this means accepting that our cultural fabric is complex and woven with many different ethnicities, and that all have something to teach us, be it a philosophy of life, medical knowledge, or a culinary dish, which adds to the richness of our personal experience.

Remember that culture is relative, and that people's social, technological and financial situations shape their way of being and looking at the world. It takes more than curiosity and tolerance to be open minded: it is a matter of learning to see the world anew, through a different cultural perspective.

When travelling abroad, don't spend too much energy looking for the familiar, and don't try to see the place as you would like it to be—go with the flow instead. And though a foreign country might seem difficult to understand or even unwelcoming at times, remember that there are people who find happiness and satisfaction in life everywhere. When you get involved in their daily lives, you will begin to see things differently—things which at first seemed exotic and mystifying are easily understood after having been explained. It always helps to know the rules before playing a game, and it goes without saying that learning the language will help you better understand what's going on. But be careful about communicating with your hands, since certain gestures might mean the opposite of what you are trying to say!

Prepare yourself for culture shock as early as possible. Libraries and bookstores are good places for information about the cultures you are interested in. Reading about them is like a journey in itself, and will leave you with even more cherished memories of your trip.

The Responsible Traveller

The adventure of travelling will probably be an enriching experience for you. But will it be the same for your hosts? The question of whether or not tourism is good for a host country is controversial. On one hand, tourism brings many advantages, such as the economic development of a region, the promotion of a culture and inter-cultural exchange; on the other hand, tourism can have negative impacts: an increase in crime, deepening of inequalities, environmental destruction, etc. But one thing is for sure: your journey will have an impact on your destination.

This is rather obvious when we speak of the environment. You should be as careful not to pollute the environment of your host country, just as you wouldn't do at home. We hear it often enough: we all live on the same planet! But when it comes to social, cultural and even economic aspects, it can be more difficult to evaluate the impact of our travels. Be aware of the reality around you, and ask

yourself what the repercussions will be before acting. Remember that you may make an impression that is much different than the one you wish to give.

Regardless of the type of travelling we choose, it is up to each and every one of us to develop a social conscience and to assume responsibility for our actions in a foreign country. Common sense, respect, altruism, and a hint of modesty are useful tools that will go a long way.

Travelling with Children

Travelling with children, however young they may be, can be a pleasant experience. A few precautions and ample preparations are the keys to a fun trip.

There are numerous activities, tours and diversions for the whole family to enjoy in St. Lucia.

In Hotels

Many hotels are well equipped for children, and there is usually no extra fee for travelling with an infant. Many hotels and bed and breakfasts have cribs; ask for one when reserving your room. You may have to pay extra for children,

Practical Information

however, but the supplement is generally low.

If you have evening plans, your hotel may be able to provide you with a list of trustworthy babysitters.

Car Rentals

Most car rental agencies rent car seats for children. They are usually not very expensive. Ask for one when making your reservation.

The Sun

Needless to say, a child's skin requires strong protection against the sun; in fact, it is preferable not to expose toddlers to its harsh rays. Before going to the beach, remember to apply sunscreen (SPF 25 for children, 35 for infants). If you think your child will spend a long time under the sun, you should consider purchasing a sunscreen with SPF 60.

Children of all ages should wear a hat that provides good coverage for the head throughout the day.

Swimming

Children usually get quite excited about playing in the waves and can do so for hours on end. However, parents must be very careful and watch them constantly; accidents can happen in a matter of seconds. Ideally, an adult should accompany children into the water, especially the younger ones, and stand farther out in the water so that the kids can play between the beach and the supervising adult. This way, he or she can quickly intervene in case of an emergency.

For infants and toddlers, some diapers are especially designed for swimming, such as "Little Swimmers" by Huggies. These are quite useful when having fun in the water!

Accommodations

St. Lucia has a large selection of accommodations that can suit any budget and sensibility. Of course, there are many sand and surf resorts but there are also a growing number of smaller establishments that offer visitors a very unique and intimate experience of St. Lucia's charms.

Price listings in this guide are based on a standard room for two people in high season. Generally, low season runs from May to December with the lowest rates available June to September.

The various services or facilities offered by each establishment are indicated with a small symbol. In no case is this an exhaustive list of what the establishment offers, but rather those we consider to be the most important. Please note that the presence of a symbol does not mean that all the rooms have this service; you sometimes have to pay extra to get, for example, a whirlpool tub. And likewise, if the symbol is not attached to an establishment, it is probably because the establishment cannot offer you this service. For a guide to the symbols used, please see the key in the first few pages of this guide.

When inquiring about a hotel's rate schedule, be sure to ask whether or not the standard 10% service charge and 8% government tax is included, in which case, tips are not necessary.

Luxury Resorts

Most of the big resort companies are represented in St. Lucia (Sandals, Hyatt, Rex and Hilton). Some are all-inclusive or offer that option. They all maintain international standards of comfort, service and security. Every activity you can

imagine is available, from scuba-diving lessons to rain forest tours. A number also have fitness centres, elegant spas and daycare facilities. Several are very upscale establishments but price ranges do vary greatly in this category.

Cottage Rentals

Instead of staying in a hotel room, many people are choosing the privacy and independence of a rented cottage or villa. Several are located on colonial estates rich in history and beautiful natural scenery. These self-contained units are also ideal for families or large groups of people.

Hotels

A wide range of styles exists, depending on your budget and preferred level of comfort. You can choose from simple, non-descript but clean rooms, much like a North American motel, to lavish suites in an upscale setting.

Guesthouses

There are no hostels in St. Lucia, so guesthouses are the most affordable option for budget travellers and backpackers. Located in each of the island's major

Practical
Information

Food Glossary

Accra
Also called fritters. Deep fried salt cod in a flour batter.

Breadfruit
A large green ball-shaped, spiny-skinned relative of the mulberry. It grows in trees and is commonly substituted for potatoes. Serve fried or boiled.

Cassava
A bitter or sweet root also known as yucca or manioc. Originally, a staple food of the Arawak Indians, it is used throughout the Caribbean. The cooked sweet variety is grated to make bread.

Christofene
A small green pear-shaped squash. The flesh is white like a potato but with a lighter and slightly sweeter flavour. Normally served fried or boiled.

Lambi
Conch fish.

Langosta
Caribbean lobster.

Pawpaw
Patois for papaya.

Provisions
Local term for side dishes in a meal. Usually salad, peas or lentils and rice or vegetables such as christofene or breadfruit.

Roti
A thin East Indian bread filled with meat or vegetables.

Saltfish
Salted codfish. A Caribbean staple for centuries.

Tablette
Coconut sugar candy.

centres, they are clean, comfortable and safe. Bathrooms and showers are shared and kitchen facilities are available. They're a great idea if you want to save money and extend your stay as long as possible.

Restaurants

There is certainly no shortage of dining options in St. Lucia. An impressive selection of world-class restaurants is available, serving everything from traditional Creole to fine continental to Chinese and Thai cuisine. Although it is possible to sample the creations of an award-winning chef, you can also excite your senses with healthy and tasty island food without spending an exorbitant amount of money. Low-, middle- and high-end budgets can all be accommodated.

Prices in this guide are based on a meal for one person, including taxes, appetizer, main course and dessert, without drinks or tips. An additional 10% service charge is standard in most restaurants and is usually included in the bill, but ask your server.

$	$10 or less
$$	$10 to $20
$$$	$20 to $30
$$$$	$30 or more

Backpackers may find meal prices in St. Lucia a bit costly compared to Asia or Africa. Cooking your own food helps offset those costs. It also gives you an opportunity to explore the many delicious fruits and vegetables found on the island.

Food

Lucian cuisine is a blend of African, East Indian, French and English influences. Each tradition has adapted to the island's diversity of plants and seafood. Take the opportunity to sample exotic tube plants like dasheen, sweet potato and African yams, which flourish in the rich volcanic soil of the southwest.

Locally grown spices like nutmeg, mace, cinnamon, cloves and ginger are available at every market, unprocessed, in their most fragrant state. You will also find fresh pineapple, grapefruit, mangoes, oranges and limes. St. Lucia's bananas are renowned for their sweetness.

Hearty callaloo soup is one of St. Lucia's most popular culinary icons. Every island in the Caribbean has its own version. Authentic Lucian callaloo is made with the leaves of the dasheen plant, rather than spinach or kale, and fortified with salted beef. Other national dishes to look out for are boiled cucumbers, pumpkin soup and fried plantain.

Practical Information

The best food bargain on the island, however, is coconut water. Besides its health properties, no other drink is as refreshing or invigorating. For $1 EC, vendors will cut the top off a green coconut and even fashion a spoon out of the husk so you can scoop out the leftover jelly inside. Look for them at every marketplace.

Drinks

St. Lucia is cocktail country. Bounty rum is produced locally and the island's own premium brand of rum is Old Fort Reserve. A selection of other Caribbean rums, like Puerto Rico's Bacardi, Barbado's Cockspur and Rhum Saint James from Martinique, is also widely available. St. Lucia's national beer is Piton and Carib is also seen all over the island. Wine is not produced on the island but stores and restaurants are generally well stocked with imported brands.

Locally grown coffee is dark and flavourful. Popular Caribbean soft drinks like Ting and ginger beer are everywhere. Restaurants and cafés always feature fresh local juices.

Taxes and Tipping

There is an 8% government tax on hotel and restaurant bills. Restaurants normally include a 10% service charge in the check. Otherwise, depending on the service, add 10 to 15% for a tip. At your discretion, feel free to tip bellhops, taxi drivers and other service people.

Shopping

High import costs mean retail items in St. Lucia tend to be expensive. The duty-free complexes at La Carenage and Point Seraphine in Castries offer good deals on a wide selection of imported clothing and jewellery.

A number of merchants sell locally made batik and clothing that are unique and beautiful. Local handicraft shops offer wood carvings, jewellery, traditional furniture and rugs made from lengths of braided grass. At markets around the island, look out for fresh spices, cocoa bars and St. Lucia's tasty hot sauces by Baron. Unfortunately, prices in the markets are for the most part fixed but always give a counter offer.

Pharmacies

Its advisable to bring an extra copy of a prescription for any essential medication just in case your drugs are lost. Pharmacies on the island are well stocked and accept credit cards.

Clarke's Drugstore, Castries
☎ *452-2727 or 452-2694*

M&C's Drugstores
JQ's Mall, Rodney Bay
☎ *458-0178*
JQ's Plaza, Vieux Fort
☎ *454-3760*
Marcellin's Pharmacy, Castries
☎ *452-1473*

Women Travellers

The question of women travelling on their own is not cut and direct. What one woman considers offensive, another may not even notice. Friendly Lucians say hello to most people, and will pay special attention to women, particularly women travelling alone. However, this attention is not generally aggressive, and ignoring it is probably your safest bet. Observe the basic safety rules for all foreign travel, and you should not have any problems. Be careful what you wear and avoid questionable or poorly lit areas, especially in urban areas.

Electricity

St. Lucia's electrical system works at 220 volts AC, 50 cycles. North American appliances need an adapter with two round pins and a converter, as do those from Britain.

Weights and Measures

Some years ago, St. Lucia officially converted to the metric system. On occasion, however, you will come across remnants of the old Imperial system.

Drugs

Marijuana is a fact of life in the Caribbean. The practice of smoking marijuana was introduced to the region after emancipation in 1838, by indentured labourers from India. Up until 1907, the British supported the practice and even profited by selling it to the colonial population.

The *ganja* grown in St. Lucia is fairly mellow. Most of the stronger *ganja* on the island actually comes from St. Vincent. Unless you're looking, how

Practical Information

Weights and Measures

Weights
1 pound (lb) = 454 grams (g)
1 kilogram (kg) = 2.2 pounds (lbs)

Linear Measure
1 inch (in) = 2.54 centimetres (cm)
1 foot (ft) = 30 centimetres (cm)
1 mile (mi) = 1.6 kilometres (km)
1 kilometre (km) = 0.63 miles (mi)
1 metre (m) = 39.37 inches (in)

Land Measure
1 acre = 0.4 hectare (ha)
1 hectare (ha) = 2.471 acres

Volume Measure
1 U.S. gallon (gal) = 3.79 litres
1 U.S. gallon (gal) = 0.8 imperial gallons

Temperature
To convert °F into °C: subtract 32, divide by 9, multiply by 5.
To convert °C into °F: multiply by 9, divide by 5, add 32.

ever, chances are you will never be approached.

Located between producers in South America and the lucrative North American market, it is no surprise that cocaine and crack have found their way onto the island. Unfortunately, this has created a few crack-head crooks who are not necessarily a physical threat but may rob tourists where they are most vulnerable, like in dark sidestreets.

Please be advised that narcotics are illegal in St. Lucia

so let common sense prevail in this regard.

Safety

Dial **911** for emergency services.

Avoid putting yourself in a vulnerable position by dressing casually and keeping a low profile with your camera, jewellery and electronic gear. Some kind of money belt or a wallet you can hang from your neck safeguards against pickpockets. At street parties or nightclubs, bring just enough money for the night, take a taxi and keep away from dark areas like the beach or deserted backstreets. In the cities, you may encounter some beggars. If you get into an uncomfortable situation with them, be firm and there should be no problem.

If you run into trouble with a thief, do not escalate the encounter. Give them whatever they want and leave quickly. Make sure you report all incidents to the local police.

The people strolling around tourist areas dressed in smart blue uniforms and berets are not paramilitaries. Officially, they are called Tourist Police, but think of them as front-line customer service representatives. If you need any kind of assistance, don't be afraid to approach them.

The Press

The Voice is a 112-year-old journalistic institution in St. Lucia. It is circulated nationally Tuesdays, Thursdays and Saturdays. Three other national weeklies are *The Crusader*, published by the ruling Labour Party, *The Mirror* and *The Star*.

Visions and *Tropical Traveller* are two very helpful publications aimed at tourists. Both are free and available at hotels and tourist board offices.

Getting Married

Many couples are choosing to wed in St. Lucia. A number of hotels, like Rendezvous St. Lucia outside Castries (**☎**452-4211, **≠**452-7419, *www.rendezvous.com.lc*), will make all the necessary legal arrangements and organize the ceremony and reception.

Requirements

Wedding couples must reside in St. Lucia three working days *(Mon-Fri)* before the ceremony. You need two witnesses, but if that's impossible, your wedding coordinator can make arrangements for someone from the island to stand in for you. Remember to bring the following original documents in English (or with an English translation): a passport valid for a minimum of six months; birth certificate; previous marriage certificate (if widowed); death certificate (if widowed); deed poll certificate (if your name has been changed); decree absolute (if divorced); parental consent (if under 18 years of age) in a notarized affidavit.

Outdoors

In recent years, St. Lucia's tourism industry has moved beyond emphasizing just the island's long stretches of warm sandy beach to promoting the natural beauty of its forest reserves, waterfalls and coral reefs.

The shift towards eco-tourism has opened up a whole range of new possibilities on the island for outdoor enthusiasts. This chapter gives an overview of the various ways in which you can enjoy St. Lucia's many exotic landscapes.

Parks

Forest Reserves

A large portion of St. Lucia's spectacular rain forest is protected in three government forest reserves: **Edmond**, **Central** and **Quilesse**. Situated in the southern interior, these reserves contain some of the island's most pristine wilderness areas and are definitely a must-see for naturalists and adventurers. A system of hiking trails in each of the reserves lets you experience this mountainous region with its waterfalls and valleys. For information regarding the forest reserves or to hire a guide, contact the forestry department (☎450-2231, ≈450-2287).

Nature Reserves

Several nature reserves are located along the southern coastline at **Maria Islands**, **Savannes Bay** and the **Frigate Islands**. These reserves protect the habitat of many birds and some extremely rare reptiles, like the St. Lucia whiptail lizard. In order to minimize the risk of damaging these ecosystems, visitor access is strictly controlled but guided tours are available at certain times of the year. Boat rides around Savannes Bay are arranged on site with local operators. The **St. Lucia National Trust** (☎452-5005) offers guided trips to the Maria Islands and visits to the Frigate Islands are organized through **Eastern Tours** (☎455-3099).

Soufrière Marine Management Area (SMMA)

Dominated by the giant Pitons, St. Lucia's southwest coast is one of the most enthralling parts of the island. Its coral reefs provide many exciting dive sites and sportfishing opportunities.

A number of sailboat moorings are also available at scenic spots along this section of the coast. The **SMMA** (P.O. Box 305, Bay St., Soufrière, ☎459-5500) was established to protect the natural resources of this unique marine environment so it can be used sustainably for both commercial and recreational purposes.

The St. Lucia National Trust

The **St. Lucia National Trust** (Clarke Ave., Vigie, ☎452-5005, ≈453-2791) is a non-profit organization devoted to preserving the island's natural and cultural heritage. This group's determination and invaluable efforts have created a number of St. Lucia's wonderful parks. Their office in Vigie is an excellent resource centre for information on the island's nature and history. The National Trust also runs guided trips to several parks, such as the Maria Islands Nature Reserve (see above), as well as a historical tour of Castries that highlights the city's major architectural landmarks.

Agouti

Outdoor Activities

Hiking

St. Lucia's efforts to promote ecotourism have resulted in the creation of a wide network of hiking trails that give visitors access to the variety of beautiful landscapes found on the island.

A large portion of the island's southern interior is divided into several forest reserves. Trails through the lush rain forest pass waterfalls, pristine rivers and open up to breathtaking vistas. Some, like the **Barre d'Isle**, follow pathways used by soldiers or escaped slaves during the earliest stages of settlement in St. Lucia. In contrast, the **East Coast Trail** meanders along the rugged windswept Atlantic shoreline through open fields of savannah and cacti. For those who appreciate altitude and the satisfaction of a demanding climb, there are trails up Gros Piton and

Mount Gimie, St. Lucia's highest point. Both reward your efforts with spectacular views and scenery that few visitors to the island experience.

All the trails are well marked and maintained, with steps built into steeper sections. The level of difficulty varies greatly from one park to the next. Some, like the **Union Nature Trail**, are more suitable for families. Others, such as the **Enbas Saut Waterfall**, involve a long climb, which is much too demanding for young children. The forestry department charges a fee to use the trails, which includes the cost of a guide; it is payable at the trailhead. You are not required to hike with a guide but they are available at the trailhead.

There are also many hiking opportunities outside the government parks. The numerous dirt roads and paths covering the island make excellent hikes; they also offer insight into rural life in St. Lucia. Should you decide to wander in backcountry areas remember, above all, to respect people's privacy and property. Whenever possible, ask

Outdoors

landowners' permission to enter their property. Trails are also set up on many estates and private parks. Many of these trails are described in the "Hiking" section of each regional chapter.

What to Bring

Lightweight hiking shoes are ideal for walks in the rain forest and a must on steep climbs like the Gros Piton Trail. To counter the intense Caribbean sun, wear sunscreen, light cotton or synthetic outdoor clothing and, if possible, a hat. For bird-watching, a pair of compact binoculars can add an interesting dimension to your hikes around the island. In the rain forest, the dense tree canopy provides some protection from the sun but humidity is an even bigger factor. If your body has not had a chance to properly adjust itself to the tropical climate, the heat and humidity can easily wear you down. The best approach is to pace yourself with frequent breaks to cool down. Bring plenty of water. Finally, keep a bathing suit handy for those opportunities along the way to cool off under a waterfall or on a secluded beach.

Swimming

By order of a royal proclamation passed by the French monarchy in the 18th century, all the beaches in St. Lucia are considered public property. Essentially, that means everyone has the right to swim on any beach they choose. Some exclusive resorts have side-stepped this law, however, by making it physically impossible for non-guests to access their beachfront. Otherwise: feel free to hit the beach!

Along St. Lucia's Caribbean coastline, the water is calmer and slightly warmer than its Atlantic side. Both have more than enough sandy beach space, but some of the best places are found at the end of an invigorating hike or an exciting jeep ride. Some sections of the east coast, like Grande Anse, experience strong ocean currents that call for a great caution. In such cases, it's best to stay as close to shore as possible or not to swim at all. In this guide, the best beaches are pointed out under the "Beaches" or "Parks and Beaches" section of each regional chapter.

Unless you're in a secluded or private area, it's best to refrain from topless sunbathing out of respect for local sensibilities.

Windsurfing

Windsurfing is growing in popularity around the island. Boards can be rented from hotels or private operators in most tourist areas. The rough and windy Atlantic coast, particularly places like Cas en Bas in the north and Anse de Sables near Vieux Fort, attracts more experienced windsurfers.

Scuba Diving and Snorkelling

The variety of dive sites and abundant marine life are two reasons why so many divers visit St. Lucia each year. The island's long history of volcanic activity has created interesting rock and coral formations which have been incorporated into a chain of dive parks along the Caribbean coastline.

Some of the best diving in the region is found off Anse La Raye and in the **Soufrière Marine Management Reserve**.

Superman's Flight, at the foot of the Petit Piton, or the wreck of the *Lesleen M* are two of the most popular dive sites. Underwater, the sea is alive with barracuda, angelfish, moray eels, octopus and seahorses swimming amongst seagrass, brain coral or large barrel sponge.

It is important to respect the vulnerability of reef ecosystems. To help protect St. Lucia's marine life and, in turn, the island's tourism industry, resist the urge to touch any fish or coral life. The government has taken steps to save this valuable resource by making it illegal to sell or posses coral products.

The excellent diving has naturally attracted many diving companies to the island. Several hotels, like Anse Chastanet (see p 178), even specialize in diving adventures. In major tourist centres, it's possible to hire guides, rent equipment or enroll in classes for advanced diving instruction or full certification. Remember to bring proof of certification and purchase holiday dive insurance.

Snorkellers can expect the same quality experience as scuba divers. A good many reefs are accessible from shore. You can also charter a boat to more remote sites. Snorkelling gear can be

Outdoors

rented at most hotels or dive centres at reasonable rates.

Horseback Riding

A unique way to explore St. Lucia's more rugged terrain is on horseback. A number of stables on the island offer professional instruction and guided trail rides through many different types of surroundings. You can saddle up and trot along the beaches and fields of the Atlantic coast, follow winding paths in the forest or enjoy an outdoor history lesson on one of the old sugar estates. Fortunately, the availability of horses for hire around the island means the only difficulty you might have is trying to decide where to ride.

Cruises and Whale-Watching

A view of St. Lucia from the water can take you back in time. Imagine how the island looked to the first Caribbean explorers, with its dramatic mountain terrain and luscious green forests. Nowadays, picturesque villages like Canaries and Anse La Raye add their charm to the coastal scenery.

Several companies run full-day or sunset cruises down the Caribbean coast to Soufrière. Tours begin in Rodney Bay or Castries and return the same day.

For an even greater adventure, whale-watching tours will bring you out into the open seas and up close to some of the earth's largest creatures. There are whales, like the humpback, and dolphins to be seen and the boat ride is a treat in itself. Trips are booked in advance and run out of Rodney Bay, Castries and Soufrière.

Golf

There are three golf courses in St. Lucia. **Club Med** in Vieux Fort and **Sandals La Toc** outside Castries both maintain excellent nine-hole facilities that are open to the public. In Cap Estate, **Golf St. Lucia** operates a beautiful 18-hole course rated at par 71.

Tennis

Most resorts have their own tennis courts. **Club St. Lucia Racquet Club** (☎*450-0106*) in Cap Estates has tennis and squash facilities along with a fully stocked pro shop, should you need to replace any equipment.

Deep-Sea Fishing

For decades, the Caribbean has been recognized as one of the best sport fishing grounds in the world. A 410kg (904lbs) marlin caught in Lucian waters still stands as one of the biggest catches on record in the region. Angling enthusiasts who visit St. Lucia can look forward to a warm tropical day fishing for sailfish, marlin, wahoo, king fish, dorado, mackerel, barracuda or tuna. Every October, the island even hosts an international billfish tournament that attracts competitors from all over the Caribbean. To get you out on the water, there are a number of qualified charter operators who offer both professional equipment and experience.

Cycling

Coasting along on the seat of a mountain bike is one of the best ways to experience St. Lucia's backcountry areas. Organized tours follow scenic routes in Cap Estates, the wild east coast or the forest regions east of Dennery.

In Soufrière, Anse Chastanet resort has created a network of trails specifically designed for mountain bikers that take you through the forest on a former sugar estate. Some of the trails are ideal for casual riders while others are geared to more advanced levels. The facilities are open to the public and all the equipment you need can be rented.

If you prefer to set your own itinerary, bike rentals are also available on the island. There is no shortage of dirt roads to follow as you leisurely explore the island's scenery.

Sailing

St. Lucia is a popular stop in the Caribbean for yacht-

Outdoors

ing enthusiasts. Wind and water conditions are ideal throughout much of the year, but the best time to sail here is November to April (see "Climate" p 58). The island hosts a number of regattas, like the famous Atlantic Rally for Cruisers in December and the Round the World Rally, which is held tri-annually.

If you are arriving by sailboat, mooring sites are located at scenic points along the Caribbean coast. The marina at Rodney Bay is exceptional, with a complete range of services available, from repairs and banks to imported groceries. It is also possible to charter boats on the island for short- or long-term use, skippered or not. Overnight voyages to Martinique or St. Vincent are easy to arrange.

Windsurfer

Rodney Bay and the North

At Pointe du Cap, on the northern tip of St. Lucia in Gros Islet Quarter, two coastlines converge into a narrow land mass pointing toward Martinique, on the other side of the St. Lucia Channel.

From this high vantage point, St. Lucia unfolds in a succession of low rounded hills and open valleys broken only by several peaks of exposed volcanic rock. Framed by the Caribbean Sea to the west, the Atlantic Ocean to the east, and the quarters of Dauphin and Castries in the south, the region of **Rodney Bay and the North** ★★ is both compact and accessible. It is also a region of intense contrasts where tourist resorts are just as much a part of the experience as solitude and exhilarating natural beauty.

Over the last decade, a profusion of hotels,

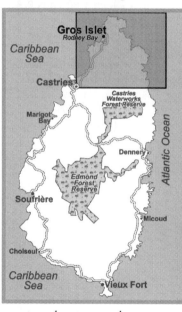

resorts and restaurants has sprung up along the Caribbean coast, particularly in Rodney Bay. An abundance of splendid beaches and hideaway coves has naturally turned this region into the island's tourism centre.

This is where most visitors come to swim, relax, sip cocktails and enjoy fine dining. The water is calm and warm and a fresh breeze from the Atlantic trade winds tempers the tropical heat and humidity. Within view of Rodney Bay's Reduit Beach is Pigeon Island National Landmark, one of St. Lucia's most significant historic sites. For centuries, the imperial destinies of Britain and France in the Caribbean depended on who possessed this strategic fortification.

On the other side of the island, the North Atlantic coastline winds and bends into secluded coves and a long stretch of beach at Cas en Bas and Anse Lavoutte all the way down to Grande Anse Bay. Stunted, twisted trees, windswept vegetation and the crash of waves against the red cliffs give this place a wild, otherworldly feel. The dense forest that once covered this

shoreline has long since disappeared and been replaced with cacti and savannah. In this open landscape, there is freedom to hike the coastline from one remote vista to the next with only curiosity as your guide.

Finding Your Way Around

Orientating yourself in the north is fairly straightforward since there's only one highway running north-south. The Castries-Gros Islet Highway parallels the Caribbean coastline from Castries past the town of Gros Islet through Cap Estate. The other major thoroughfare is the Babonneau Highway, which branches east from the main Castries-Gros Islet Highway near Choc Beach, forming a loop around the north-central regions through Babonneau, Paix Bouche and Monchy. Most of the surfaced and unsurfaced secondary roads branching out from the axis of these two

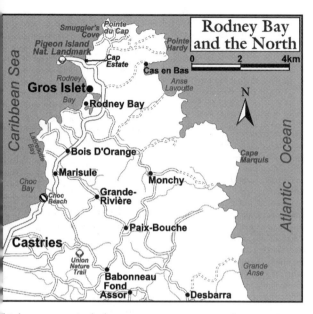

highways, particularly on the Reduit Peninsula in Rodney Bay, are not named, which can lead to some confusion.

By Car

All the major car rental agencies have outlets in the Rodney Bay area. There are three gas stations along the main highway: one at the turnoff for Gros Islet, another just south of Rodney Bay and one further south in Bois D'Orange.

Car Rental Agencies

H & B Car Rental Agency
☎452- 0872

Avis
☎462-9560

Cool Breeze Jeep - Car Rental
☎458-0824

Courtesy Car Rental
☎452-8140 or 450-8140

Hertz
☎452-0679

By Bus

Minibuses run frequently along the main highway

Rodney Bay and the North

between Castries to the centre of Gros Islet and Babonneau Highway. If you need to go any further north it will cost you extra so make sure you discuss the price beforehand. The fare from Gros Islet to Castries is $1.50.

By Taxi

Taxis can be booked for single trips or for a flat half or full-day rate. Government regulation has eliminated the excitement (or exasperation) of negotiating the price of a ride by setting fares according to an island standard. Every taxi should have a rate sheet available if for some reason you feel unsure about a driver's price.

Taxi Services

North Lime Taxi Service
☎452-8562

Rainbow Taxi Service
☎458-0389

Rodney Bay Taxi Service
☎452-0379

Pigeon Point Northern Taxi Service
☎450-9069

By Boat

Ferries operate regularly from Rodney Bay to Pigeon Island, Gros Islet and the marina. Budget travellers may find the $10 ticket to Pigeon Island a bit pricey, but the short trip offers a wonderful view of this historic inlet. Ferries depart daily from Rodney Bay at 10am, 11am, noon, 1pm and 2pm. Two operators have set up kiosks in the heart of Rodney Bay across from the Rex Papillion Hotel beside the Lime Restaurant. They also hire out water taxis to points along the west coast.

West Coast Ferry
☎452-8079

Rodney Bay Ferry
☎452-0087

Practical Information

Rodney Bay

Post Office

Mon-Fri 9am to noon and 1pm to 5pm
JQ Charles Mall next to the unmistakable Kentucky Fried Chicken outlet

Supermarkets

Julians
Mon-Thu 8am to 10pm; Fri and Sat 8am to midnight; Sun 8am to 4pm
on the main highway north of the Rodney Bay junction

Le Marche de France
Mon-Sat 8am to 9pm; Sun 8am to 1pm
in the Rodney Bay Marina Pl.

Tourist Information

There are no government tourism offices in this region since travel information is so readily available from hotels, car-rental agencies and tour operators.

Banks

Barclays
Rodney Bay Marina Pl.

Royal Bank of Canada
Rodney Bay Marina Pl.

Scotiabank
across from Dominos pizza in the centre of Rodney Bay

Gros Islet

Post Office

Mon-Fri 9am to noon and 1pm to 5pm
Church St. by the cemetery at the north end of town

Supermarkets

There are several small grocery shops situated around the intersection of Dauphine and Bridge streets.

Exploring

There are two tours in this chapter. **Tour A ★★★** begins in Rodney Bay and passes through Gros Islet on the way to the northern tip of the island at Pointe du Cap, and then explores the upper sections of the Atlantic coastline. **Tour B ★★** to Grande Anse brings you through the central interior to remote bays and coves on the Atlantic coast.

★★★

Tour A:
Rodney Bay, Gros Islet
and Pointe du Cap

Rodney Bay

Our first tour begins on the main highway from Castries in **Rodney Bay ★★**, which is not actually a town but a dense concentration of hotels, restaurants, nightclubs and condominiums. A turnoff at the large JQ Charles Mall leads you onto

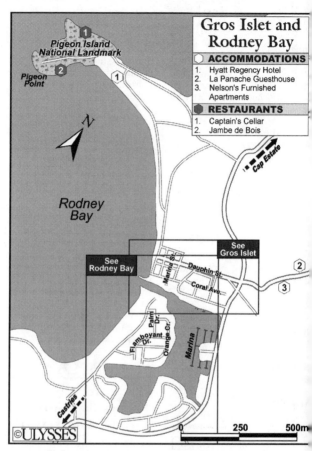

Gros Islet and Rodney Bay

ACCOMMODATIONS
1. Hyatt Regency Hotel
2. La Panache Guesthouse
3. Nelson's Furnished Apartments

RESTAURANTS
1. Captain's Cellar
2. Jambe de Bois

Pigeon Island National Landmark

Pigeon Point

Rodney Bay

Cap Estate

See Gros Islet

See Rodney Bay

Marina St.

Dauphin St.

Coral Ave.

Palm Dr.

Flamboyant Dr.

Orange Cr.

Marina

Castries

©ULYSSES

0   250   500m

Reduit Peninsula, St. Lucia's tourist hub. Here, you'll find restaurants preparing everything from Creole-style chicken and English pub fare to Thai or Continental cuisine. Amongst the many hotels and resorts, are tour operators, car-rental agencies and souvenir shops. Developers were initially seduced to this area by **Reduit Beach ★★★** (see p 99), a wide arch of fine sand and placid water. During the Second World War, the U.S. Marine Corps maintained a naval air station at Rodney Bay, one of several posts in the Caribbean charged with protecting ships from South America

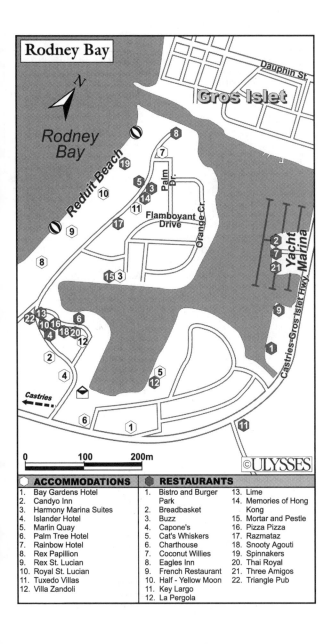

Rodney Bay

Rodney Bay

Gros Islet

Dauphin St.

Reduit Beach

Palm Dr.

Flamboyant Drive

Orange Cr.

Yacht Marina

Castries–Gros Islet Hwy.

← Castries

0   100   200m

©ULYSSES

ACCOMMODATIONS	RESTAURANTS	
1. Bay Gardens Hotel	1. Bistro and Burger Park	13. Lime
2. Candyo Inn	2. Breadbasket	14. Memories of Hong Kong
3. Harmony Marina Suites	3. Buzz	15. Mortar and Pestle
4. Islander Hotel	4. Capone's	16. Pizza Pizza
5. Marlin Quay	5. Cat's Whiskers	17. Razmataz
6. Palm Tree Hotel	6. Charthouse	18. Snooty Agouti
7. Rainbow Hotel	7. Coconut Willies	19. Spinnakers
8. Rex Papillion	8. Eagles Inn	20. Thai Royal
9. Rex St. Lucian	9. French Restaurant	21. Three Amigos
10. Royal St. Lucian	10. Half - Yellow Moon	22. Triangle Pub
11. Tuxedo Villas	11. Key Largo	
12. Villa Zandoli	12. La Pergola	

carrying resources for the Allied war effort against German U-boats. A short walk out to the west section of the bay and you'll find the old American bunkers that were built into the side of Mount Pimard. They still look defiant, albeit over-grown and forgotten.

Before Rodney Bay became the tourism centre it is to-day, enormous efforts were undertaken to transform this former mangrove swamp. The marina and harbour were created only 30 years ago, after a decision to flood the swamp.

Gros Islet

Back at the highway junc-tion, a left turn brings you around the harbour across a flat plain to the town of **Gros Islet** ★. At the gas station, turn left onto Dau-phine Street, which takes you through town and down to the water. Origi-nally, the old Castries-Gros Islet Road followed Reduit Beach across a wooden bridge over a small river and into the centre of Gros Islet via Bridge Street. Now giant catamarans and yachts sail by in the gulf that di-vides both shores. The physical disconnection from the tourist scene in Rodney Bay has allowed Gros Islet to keep a measure of its

traditional identity as a Creole fishing village.

The rows of traditional wooden homes near the waterfront are a glimpse at scenes from this village's past. At the corner of Bridge and Church streets is the **Church of St. Joseph the Worker** ★. Built in 1926, its design is typical of Roman Catholic churches around St. Lucia and other French Caribbean islands.

To continue, either follow Dauphine Street to the beach where it becomes Bay Street and take the dirt road towards **Causeway Beach** ★ (see p 99) or re-turn to the highway, and turn left further north at the sign for Pigeon Island. A quieter alternative to Reduit Beach, Causeway Beach mostly attracts locals from Gros Islet and the odd stray tourist. For visitors, the name Pigeon Island seems like a misnomer. But 30 years ago a land bridge was built to connect the island with the mainland, creating Causeway Beach.

Head back to the highway, turn left, and take the turn-off for **Pigeon Island National Landmark** ★★★ *($10; every day 9am to 5pm;* ☎*450-8167)* a short distance ahead. St. Lucia's expansive mili-tary history is tied very closely to this former island fortress. A tour provides an

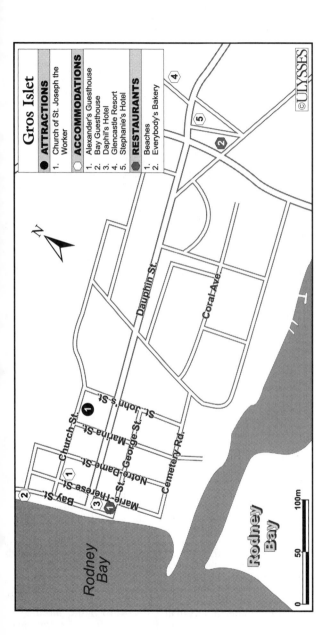

Gros Islet

● ATTRACTIONS
1. Church of St. Joseph the Worker

○ ACCOMMODATIONS
1. Alexander's Guesthouse
2. Bay Guesthouse
3. Daphil's Hotel
4. Glencastle Resort
5. Stephanie's Hotel

● RESTAURANTS
1. Beaches
2. Everybody's Bakery

© ULYSSES

Rodney Bay

Rodney Bay

Bay St.
Marie-Thérèse St.
Church St.
Notre-Dame St.
Marina St.
George St.
St. John's St.
Cemetery Rd.
Dauphin St.
Coral Ave.

0   50   100m

opportunity to imagine what life was like for a British soldier unfortunate enough to have been stationed in the West Indies during the 18th century. Climb up the two peaks as frigate birds and pelicans fly by at eye level. From the higher signal station, word of incoming French warships from Martinique would have been communicated to an excited governor at a similar station faintly visible on the top of Morne Fortune. The panoramic view of the island and the Caribbean Sea is worth the effort of getting to the top. In

Gros Islet Church

a restored barracks, the St. Lucia National Trust maintains a small but informative museum describing Pigeon Island's varied history as a British fort, U.S. communications post, whaling station and finally as the secluded home of an English socialite. There are also two restaurants and a small beach.

Back at the main junction, turn left towards **Cap Estate ★★**. In the early days of colonization, this area's moderate terrain and dark, fertile soil attracted farmers who grew tobacco, indigo or cotton. When the sugar boom took over the economy of the Caribbean in the 19th century, farmers vigorously cleared the tall forests that once covered the north in order to plant cane. At that time, the countryside was a patchwork of sugar-cane fields. During the harvest, African slaves were busy in the fields cutting cane and piling it onto carts, while rings of smoke rose from the mills where the cane juice was being boiled to make sugar. A master's house would not have been far away, and beside it, a cluster of huts with their own small subsistence gardens for the slaves.

Driving northward, the road curves only slightly through a very different landscape. Just as the forests have disappeared, so too have the plantations. A combination of overplanting and the eroding forces of wind and water devastated the soil. Nowadays, a few horses and cattle graze amidst the scrub brush and brown fields that rise gently into sloping hills. The plantations have been replaced by large villas, holiday resorts and an 18-hole golf course.

A short distance past the exclusive residences of Cap Estate, on the left, a long, tree-lined driveway leads to the illustrious **Great House ★**, former home of Monsieur de Longueville, France's military commandant for St. Lucia in the middle of the 18th century. Hurricanes and revolutionary fires destroyed the original estate house, but it has been restored and converted into a fine restaurant (see p 116). A stroll on the grounds gives you a sense of the elegance and grandeur of elite colonial life.

At the three-way junction further up the highway, take the middle road marked Saline Point, which ultimately leads to the far northern tip of the island and **Pointe du Cap ★★★**. As the road steepens, asphalt gives way to a smooth concrete surface that eventually breaks down into a rough pot-holed track worthy of a four-wheel-drive vehicle. Its really not that long a hike so whenever it seems like your vehicle has reached its limit, find a place to pull over and walk up to the

top. The large, modern residential properties on either side of the road reveal this is one of the more affluent areas of the island. Vehicles are barred from the lookout but there is space to park by the chain gate.

Pointe du Cap is located at the end of a long red-dirt track. A rickety old gazebo stands in spite of the strong wind, and clumps of thornbrush here and there are visited by finches, golden doves and yellow butterflies. The breathtaking panorama encompasses the northern tip of the island; Pointe Hardy can be seen reaching out into the Atlantic Ocean to the east, and to the west, by the Caribbean Sea, is Rodney Bay and Pigeon Island. On a clear day you can see the south of Martinique.

From Pointe du Cap, the nearest beach is no more than 10min away at **Smuggler's Cove ★** (see p 99). To get there, make a right at the three-way junction onto the road leading past Le Sport Resort. On your right, you'll see a path with stairs leading down to the water.

Heading south on the highway back to Rodney Bay, the road to **Cas en Bas ★★★** (see p 99) is on the left, opposite Dauphine

Rodney Bay and the North

Street, which heads to Gros Islet. The journey to this secluded beach, along a rough dirt track, is an exciting adventure in itself. The drive starts with a fairly decent asphalt road that gradually deteriorates into pot-holes and broken pavement before turning into a dirt track, impassable in certain sections with anything other than a four-wheel-drive vehicle, especially during rainy season. Simple concrete homes line the road amidst parched fields, short dusty trees and tall coconut palms. Stick to the main road all the way down into the bay area of Cas en Bas.

To return to Rodney Bay, take the same dirt road and turn left at the Castries-Gros Islet Highway.

★★★

Tour B: Grande Anse

To begin, follow the Castries-Gros Islet Highway south from Rodney Bay through **Bois D'Orange** to a sharp bend on the right towards **Choc Bay**. A signpost on the right for the East Winds Inn will lead you to **Labrelotte Bay ★★**, a shel-

tered inlet lined with a fine sand beach that is much quieter and more secluded than Reduit Beach. Wash-rooms and drinks are available nearby and since the beach is used by hotel guests, it is maintained regularly.

Agouti

Further down the main highway, before an abrupt curve to the left, away from Choc Bay, is a road that takes you to **Choc Beach ★★** (see p 100), a long strip of fine sand that's great for swimming.

Retrace your steps and head north a short distance to the big intersection and make a right onto the Babonneau Highway. Less than 1km (0.5mi) later, the road gradually steepens as it winds up the valley alongside the Choc River. After the LUCELEC electrical plant, turn right at the Gabriel Charles Forestry Complex. On the other side of the bridge, another quick right turn leads you to the **Union**

Nature Trail and Mini Zoo ★ ★ *($10; Mon-Fri 9am to 4pm, on weekends no guides are available, just pay the gate attendant, ☎450-2231)*. The Department of Forest and Lands originally used this area as a tree nursery for reforestation projects on the island. The terrain is moderate and the inclusion of a short-cut loop makes this one of the few hiking trails on the island small children can enjoy.

The park also operates a mini zoo that offers a close look at most of the island's bigger fauna like agouti, iguana and the St. Lucia parrot. In spite of limited resources, staff keep the animals healthy and the cages well maintained. For plant enthusiasts, there is a garden display of herbs used in local medicine and a nursery with many of the island's different trees including some very exotic pine species.

Old sugar-cane press

Next, turn right and continue east on the highway into the Babonneau district. Known for its many rivers, this region supplies a large portion of the island's fresh water. As you travel deeper into the valley, mountains begin to cut across the horizon, covered with a layer of thick, green vegetation. In the town of Babonneau, turn left at the first junction onto a road that follows a ridge just below Mount Chaubourg to the east. Though Lucians claim Empress Josephine, the exalted wife of Napoleon Bonaparte, was born on a plantation nearby in Morne Paix Bouche, the evidence points to the island of Martinique as her actual place of birth.

The road descends into a beautiful valley formerly owned by the Marquis Estate. In the late 18th century, this was one of St. Lucia's wealthiest plantations. An abundance of fertile land and the strong currents from the Marquis River provided early French planters with irrigation and energy to turn the gigantic wheels of their sugar mills.

Down a rough 5km (3mi) track on the left is **Marquis Estate**. The old estate house has been maintained and still reflects its once grand past as the much-coveted home of former French governors. Through the historical tides of plummeting sugar prices, hurricanes, the end of slavery and falling banana prices, the plantation has been subdivided and even reinvented as a tourist attraction. Unfortunately, tours are no longer available, so you'll have to content yourself with a look from the outside.

After crossing the Marquis River bridge, our route swerves to the right through banana plantations and the **Castries Waterworks Forest Reserve**, a watershed area that provides this region with much of its water. At the top of a pass, perched at the foot of La Sorciere, the highest peak in the region, is the small village of **Desbarra**.

Keep to the left on a dirt track, past a rough backcountry soccer field, until you reach the gate to **Grande Anse ★★★**. There is no charge to enter but a security guard will take down your license plate number to make sure you return safely. A watchperson on duty 24hrs a day is also needed to protect the fine-sand on the beach from sand poachers, nocturnal environmental bandits who are in part responsible for the substantial shrinkage of the beach.

Our route follows a slope down the other side of the island into a wide valley that ends at the Atlantic Ocean. As you approach the bottom, the expansive views take in the tall ridges that cradle this inlet and form sharp rocky points at the coast. Above the western horizon is the impressive summit of La Sorciere. Archaeological finds have indicated this valley was the site a substantial Arawak settlement around AD 600. Though the track becomes increasingly difficult, the real challenge is crossing two riverbeds making a four-wheel-drive vehicle an absolute necessity for this part of the tour.

Grande Anse is a remote strip of luxuriously fine sand renowned as much for its natural beauty as it is for the pregnant sea turtles that come here to nest each year. Remember to park your vehicle far away from the beach to avoid crushing any eggs buried below the surface. The water here is rough and the authorities advise against swimming, but this is a great area to explore on foot. At the north end, a path at the base of a rocky bluff leads across Tanti Point to Petite Anse. Though this inlet is less exposed than Grande Anse, there are still dangerous currents close to shore. While you're walking along the beach, watch for large round depressions or tracks in the sand left by sea turtles.

Return to Rodney Bay using the same route.

Parks and Beaches

★★★

Reduit Beach

Located in Rodney Bay, the beach here is long enough to find your own space and not feel too crowded in spite of the many tourists in the area. Public access points are located at the north and south ends of the beach for those who are not staying at one of the seaside hotels. Several restaurants are located nearby along with a rental shop for scuba gear, windsurfing boards, sunfish sailboats and thrilling watersports like parasailing and waterskiing.

Causeway Beach

Near Gros Islet, this beach has a somewhat rougher quality compared to the well-maintained beach next door at the Hyatt Regency, but it offers the same water and you needn't feel obliged to buy a drink at Hyatt prices. Although the recent construction of the Hyatt Regency hotel has cut a fair chunk of the shoreline, much of it is still accessible to the general public.

Smuggler's Cove

Tucked between two tall cliffs, this small picturesque beach in Cap Estate is a great spot for snorkellers as well as sun worshippers. The sense of seclusion would be complete were it not for the stream of guests from the nearby Club St. Lucia and the seductive refreshments bar.

Cas en Bas

This remote north Atlantic inlet is a wide bay shaped like a bent horseshoe covered with a long gray strip of sand. Two rocky promontories jut out into the Atlantic Ocean at each end, providing shelter from the rough waters. Cas en Bas is wonderful for swimming and it's also an ideal spot to begin exploring St. Lucia's rugged northeast coast.

Rodney Bay and the North

River in the north, Choc Beach attracts locals and tourists alike to its calm water and palm-tree-lined shore. At the lively Waves Beach Bar, you can drink sunset cocktails or rent water toys like windsurfing boards, sunfish sailboats or kayaks.

Outdoor Activities

Cruises

Catamaran cruises down the Caribbean coast are very popular. The boats stop along the way for a bit of snorkelling, swimming and rum punch before continuing on to Soufrière to visit some local attractions. Groups tend to be rather large but this is certainly a fun and carefree way to spend the day out on the water.

Cats Limited
☎450-8651

Mango Tango
☎452-8232

Glass Bottom Cruises
☎450-0033

Swimming in the Atlantic is different from the Caribbean Sea. Here, you sense the wind blowing and the waves rocking the sea. In some of the smaller coves further north and south, the currents are very unpredictable, so if you choose to go in, stay close to shore. An enterprising young vendor may have a cooler full of drinks available on the beach, but it's best to bring enough water for the day, especially if you're hiking in from the main highway or exploring the coastline.

Choc Beach

On the Caribbean Sea, bounded by Vide Bouteille Point in the south and Choc

Deep-Sea Fishing

Mako Watersports
☎*452-0412*
If you're interested in trying to catch a trophy-size marlin or sailfish, Mako Watersports in Rodney Bay offers full-and half-day charters.

Golf

St. Lucia Golf and Country Club
☎*450-8523*
Located in Cap Estate, the 18-hole St. Lucia Golf and Country Club is the only golf course in the region.

Hiking

The starting point for some of the best hiking in this part of the island is found at the end of the road to **Cas en Bas**, on the Atlantic coast. A number of paths worn in by fishers and livestock meander along the coast in both directions. The forest pulled away from the shoreline long ago and in its place is a sparse landscape of exposed volcanic rock, short twisted trees and patches of cacti. The openness of the land and the cool Atlantic breeze make this a wonderful place to simply wander and follow your curiosity—but bring water.

If you decide to head north towards Pointe Hardy, save yourself a lot of unnecessary climbing by following the smaller path that veers to the right and traverses the promontory lower down. No more than 2km (1.25mi) away is the solitude of Anse du Banc. Moving south, the long trek around Giromon Point is amply rewarded by the views off Comorette Point at the end of a long sandy beach. Further south is Rouge Point and tiny Lapins Island.

Union Nature Trail and Mini Zoo
$10
Mon-Fri 9am to 4pm, on weekends no guides are available, just pay the gate attendant
☎*450-2231*
The Union Nature Trail and Mini Zoo near Babonneau, is a relatively short hike that is suitable for children. The park has a strong educational component that teaches visitors about native flora and fauna. Signs identifying different plants in the forest are posted along a compact network of trails that passes through mature plantations of mahogany,

Rodney Bay and the North

blue mahoe, teak and Caribbean pine.

Horseback Riding

This is a popular area for riding, with several stables offering professional instruction, healthy steeds and guided trail rides along the east coast and over to Gros Islet as well as the Babonneau region.

International Riding Stables
☎452-8139

Fayole Riding Stables
☎458-2229

Trims National Riding Stable
☎450-8273

Four-Wheel-Drive Tours

ATV Adventures
☎452-6441
ATV Adventures offers guided tours of the countryside southeast of Babonneau in four-wheel all-terrain vehicles. No special license is required and drivers must be at least 12 years of age.

Safari Fun Drive
☎452-8232
Safari Fun Drive takes you in an eight-wheeled all-terrain vehicle from Pointe

du Cap along the scenic Atlantic coastline to Cas en Bas.

Jungle Tours (☎450-0434) and **Jeep Safari** (☎452-0459) let you see the island from the back of an open jeep on your way to Soufrière and hikes in the rain forest.

Sailing

Every November, Rodney Bay welcomes participants in the Atlantic Rally for Cruisers upon their arrival from the Canary Islands. The **Rodney Bay Marina** (☎452-8411) is one of the best sailing facilities in the Caribbean. The centre is equipped with a complete range of shore facilities for groceries, telecommunications, sail and engine repairs and banking services. A number of sailboat charters are based here, offering trips ranging from half-day cruises around St. Lucia to long-term island hopping excursions. The marina's administrative office can provide information and a comprehensive list of local charter outfits. Here are a few:

Dinask
☎484-7060

Villa Zandoli
☎452-8898

Stirrup Yachts
☎*452-8000*

Scuba Diving

There is one dive site off the coast of Smuggler's Cove and another in Cas en Bas. Further down the Caribbean coast are sites near Labrellotte Point and the north end of Choc Bay at Masson Point. You can obtain instruction, boats and equipment at **Scuba St. Lucia** (☎*452-8009*) or at **Buddies Scuba Limited** (☎*452-9086*). Both are located in Rodney Bay.

Tennis

If your hotel does not have tennis courts, the **St. Lucia Racquet Club** (☎*450-0106*) in Cap Estate has nine first-class courts, seven of which are lit up at night. Facilities also include squash courts, professional instructors and a pro shop.

Water Sports

On Reduit Beach, water thrills like parasailing, waterskiing and tube rides are available from **Scuba St. Lucia** (☎*452-8009*) and on

Choc Beach from **Waves Beach Bar** (☎*451-3000*).

Windsurfing

Many experienced windsurfers are drawn to the wind and waves of the Atlantic coast but choose the more sheltered environment of Cas en Bas. For a less intense experience more suitable for beginners, Rodney Bay and Choc Bay are popular. Boards and instruction are available from **Scuba St. Lucia** (☎*452-8009*) on Reduit Beach or at **Waves Beach Bar** (☎*451-3000*) at Choc Beach. Further north, there is Smugglers' Cove and the area surrounding Saline Point.

Turtle-Watching

St. Lucia Naturalist Society
☎*452-8900 or 422-9829 evenings*
For the past 17 years, the St. Lucia Naturalist Society has been monitoring the number of sea turtles visiting Grande Anse during the egg-laying season between March and July. Volunteers are welcome to help collect valuable data on such endangered species as the giant leatherback turtle (see p 16) and with patrols on the beach to deter poachers. The chances of actually

seeing a turtle are quite good and a night under the stars on a remote Caribbean beach is worthwhile in itself.

Participants alternate between watching for turtles and sleeping in tents provided by the society. All you need to bring are sneakers, warm clothes, food, drinks and a flashlight. Its necessary to call and book a spot in advance. Everyone meets in front of the central library in downtown Castries on Saturday at 4pm and leaves Grande Anse the following morning at 6am *($26; Mar to July)*.

Accommodations

Rodney Bay, Gros Islet and Pointe du Cap

Rodney Bay

Villa Zandoli
$144 bkfst incl.
⊗, ℝ, *K, sb*
P.O. Box 1538, Gros Islet, south side of the street, second right when you enter Reduit
☎*452-8898*
⇄*452-0093*
www.saintelucie.com
Run by French Canadians, Villa Zandoli is the most

affordable accommodation in Rodney Bay. Rooms are simple but clean and the common area is open and comfortable. Though very accessible to nightlife and the beach, the guesthouse is set back far enough from the action so you can still enjoy its quiet atmosphere.

Bay Gardens Hotel
$200
≡, ≈, ⊛, ℜ
P.O. Box 1892 Castries north side of Castries-Gros Islet Hwy. 1 block west of JQ Charles Mall
☎*452-8060*
⇄*452-8059*
baygardens@candw.lc
A 10min walk from Reduit Beach, Bay Gardens Hotel offers clean, comfortable rooms with modern amenities in a classy but unpretentious atmosphere. The soft-coloured wood and wicker furnishings mixed with the bright floral designs give the rooms a cheery ambiance. Families will appreciate the ample green space around the property.

Islander Hotel
$221
≡, ≈, ℜ, ℝ, *K*
P.O. Box 907, Castries east side of the first street on your left after you enter Reduit
☎*452-8757*
⇄*452-0958*
For the money, the Islander Hotel offers more than just decent accommodation. Being one of the older ho-

tels in Reduit, it may seem slightly tarnished but the staff is friendly and attentive. The rooms are laid out with the kitchen and common area next to a patio decorated with lots of plants. Set back from the main road, the huge courtyard has plenty of green space, which id great for children. Reduit Beach is two blocks away.

Palm Tree Hotel
$223
≡, ≈, ⊛, ℜ, ⊘, ℝ
P.O. Box 2233, Gros Islet north side of Castries-Gros Islet Hwy. beside JQ Charles Mall
☎*452-8200*
⇄*452-8894*
www.palmtreestlucia.com
The Palm Tree Hotel provides visitors with comfortable rattan-style furniture. Their best feature is the private balcony, with glass doors and wood trimming, which overlooks the pool.

Rainbow Hotel
$260
≡, ⊗, ≈, ℜ, ⊘
P.O. Box 3050, La Clery, Castries, Palm Dr. north end of Reduit.
☎*452-0148*
⇄*452-0158*
rainbow@candw.lc
Seventy-six rooms surround the Rainbow Hotel's beautiful courtyard with its lush tropical plants, bright flowers and large swimming pool. The rooms have rattan furniture and white tile floors, and the environment

is modern, clean and pleasant. If you want a change from the tile patio, the northern tip of Reduit Beach is just a quick 2min walk across the street.

Harmony Marina Suites
$288
≡, ≈, ℜ, ℝ, K, ◉
P.O. Box 155 Castries, Flamboyant Dr. west of the Rex Hotel
☎*452-8756*
⇄*452-8677*
harmony@candw.lc
Twenty successful years in the business means Harmony Suites is experienced in providing thoroughly professional service. Boat berths are available which makes it popular among sea-weary sailors looking for a cozy well-furnished room on dry land. There are not many hotels on the island that offer one bedroom suites at this rate with a fully equipped kitchen and all the amenities. The atmosphere is quiet and relaxing and Reduit Beach is only a short walk away from your private balcony or patio.

Marlin Quay
$295
≡, ≈, ℜ, ℝ, K
P.O. Box 2204, on the waterfront north of the Castries-Gros Islet Hwy. behind Julian's supermarket
☎*452-0393*
⇄*452-0383*
www.marlin-quay.com
The pleasant pueblo-style architecture of the Marlin

Quay is tailor-made for those who enjoy soaking up the sun. The spacious courtyard decorated with palm frond shelters includes two pools and a children's area. Besides a generous balcony, these rooms are bright with plenty of natural light and enlivened with a stylish decor that includes hardwood furniture, terra cotta floors and several plants. There are several boat berths and the hotel provides complimentary ferry rides for day trips to Reduit Beach.

Rex St. Lucian
$576

≡, ≈, ⊛, ℜ, ☺

P.O. Box 512, Castries, middle hotel on Reduit Beach

☎*452-8351*

⇄*452-8331*

www.rexcaribbean.com

In spite of being the lowest priced Rex resort on Reduit Beach, the Rex St. Lucian is still considered luxurious by any standards. Long, spacious rooms overlooking the beach and swimming pool, along with a very tasteful decor provide guests with a classy but cozy environment. Patrons of all three Rex hotels also have access to many of the same facilities.

Rex Papillion
$789 all incl. (min. three nights)

≡, ⊗, ≈, ⊛, ℜ, ☺

P.O. Box 512, Castries, first hotel at the south end of Reduit Beach

☎*452-0984*

⇄*452-9332*

www.rexcaribbean.com

Originally built in 1969, Rex Resorts revamped the St. Lucia Hotel into a luxurious and stylish resort called the Papillion. Each of its spacious rooms has a sitting area inside and a table on the balcony overlooking beautiful Reduit Beach. A window with wooden shutters lets you enjoy the fresh seabreeze. The grounds are, of course, impeccable and the service is what you would expect from an upscale hotel chain. One of only three beachfront hotels in Rodney Bay.

🏝 Royal St. Lucian
$1,013 all incl. (min. three nights)

≡, ⊗, ≈, ⊛, ℜ, ☺, ◧

P.O. Box 977, Castries, last hotel at the north end of Reduit Beach

☎*452-9999*

⇄*452-9639*

www.rexcaribbean.com

The Royal St. Lucian is the most expensive accommodation in Reduit. Classical music in the background, a water fountain in the lobby and a long winding staircase are some of the details that give this hotel its refined atmosphere. Suites have separate bedrooms, luxurious bathrooms and large sitting rooms with elegant rattan furniture and plenty of soft cushions. All the rooms have balconies overlooking Reduit Beach and the hotel's unique freshwater pool. A full service spa is also available.

Gros Islet

Alexander's Guesthouse
$78
⊗, ℝ, *K*, *sb*
Marie Therese St., half block north of Dauphine St.
☎*450-8610*
⇄*450-8014*
Located less than 100m (328ft) from Causeway Beach, Alexander's Guesthouse is pervaded by a friendly, family-style atmosphere. This is one of few options for budget travellers in the north. The rooms are well kept, if a little cramped with furniture, but there is a communal kitchen and lounge on the main floor for socializing.

Bay Guesthouse
$78
⊗, ℝ, *K*
Bay St., on the beach road at the end of Dauphine St. west of Marie Therese St.
☎/⇄*450-8956*
www.geocities.com/TheTropics/Cabana/7071/
German owned, the Bay Guesthouse offers visitors several uniquely designed rooms looking out onto Rodney Bay and Pigeon Island. The wood fixtures

and tropical decor create a cozy beach house sort of ambiance. The centre of Gros Islet and Causeway Beach are right next door, yet there is still plenty of private green space to spread out on and relax by the water.

Daphil's Hotel
$85
⊗, ℜ
West side Marie Therese St., south of Dauphine St.
☎*450-9318*
⇄*452-4387*
Daphil's Hotel has clean, functional rooms in the heart of Gros Islet. The building may have a slightly institutional look from the outside, but it offers ample privacy and the staff is friendly and helpful. Patrons have access to kitchen facilities along with a common room and two balconies.

La Panache Guesthouse
$85
⊗, ℝ, *K*
P.O Box 2074, Gros Islet, 2km (1.2mi) down Cas en Bas Rd., north side
☎*450-0765*
⇄*450-0453*
www.cavip.com/en/botels/lapanache.html
The location of La Panache and its natural surroundings make it ideal for travellers who wish to explore St. Lucia's northern landscape. The huge rooms, which come with basic furnishings and a full kitchen,

are great for families. There is also plenty of green space on the property and a funky terrace lounge where the atmosphere is typically fun, casual and friendly.

Nelson's Furnished Apartments
$99

⊗, ℝ, *K*

P.O. Box 1174, Castries, 3km (1.5mi) down Cas en Bas Rd., south side

☎ *450-8275*

⇻ *450-9108*

Nelson's Furnished Apartments are quiet, self-contained and private. This is not so much a vacation spot as a home away from home for anyone planning to stay for an extended period. All these ample-size rooms have views of Rodney Bay Marina and the beach at Cas en Bas is only a short hike away.

Glencastle Resort
$195

≡, ≈, ℜ

P.O. Box 143, Castries, first left on the road to Cas en Bas, right-hand side

☎ *450-0833*

⇻ *450-0873*

www.st-lucia.de

One of Glencastle Resort's best features is the view of Rodney Bay and the marina from the balcony. The staff's warm, professional manner, combined with ample pool and patio space, make this an easy place to relax. The 37 rooms have tasteful wood furnishings but could be a bit larger. Though situated

on the outskirts of the tourist scene in Rodney Bay, the Glencastle Resort offers quiet surroundings and there is a free shuttle to Reduit or Pigeon Island.

Hyatt Regency
$975

≡, ≈, ⊛, ℜ, ⊘, ◉

P.O. Box 2247, Gros Islet, Pigeon Island Causeway

☎ *451-1234*

⇻ *450-9450*

www.stlucia.hyatt.com

The Hyatt's imposing presence across the mid-section of Causeway Beach sets it apart from other hotels in the north. There's no denying its impressive facilities and beautiful rooms, but its huge proportions give it an impersonal atmosphere. All the rooms have plenty of space both inside and out on their private balconies. The furnishings are elegant, very comfortable and you can expect such classy details as a hair dryer, heated mirror and double sinks. This is also a popular venue for business meetings and conferences.

Cap Estate

Hotel Capri
$125

≡, ≈, ℜ

P.O. Box 1296, Castries, left at the three way junction, facing Le Sport Hotel

☎ *450-0009*

⇻ *450-0180*

Hotel Capri is much smaller than the other hotels in Cap

Estate, which makes for a more private experience. In addition to offering lovely views of Smuggler's Cove, the rooms are very spacious and attractively furnished with plenty of windows you can actually open! Patrons can use the swimming pool or walk across the street to Le Sport Beach.

Le Sport
$806 all incl.
≡, ≈, ⊛, ℜ, ⊘, ▣

P.O. Box 437, Castries, left at the three way junction on the main Cap Estate road

☎ 450-8551
≈ 450-0368
www.lesport.com.lc

Upscale, luxurious and elegant, Le Sport is situated in a secluded cove near the rocky bluff of Saline Point. Bright and very comfortable, all the rooms have private balconies with views of the Caribbean Sea and offer the refined styling of a king-size four poster bed and Italian marble baths. In every sense, the focus here is on health, fitness and relaxation. Patrons have access to all sorts of interesting activities, including tai chi, meditation, aerobics, windsurfing and scuba diving.

Club St. Lucia
$775 all incl.
≡, ≈, ℜ, ⊘, ▣

P.O. Box 915, Castries, left at the three-way junction on the main Cap Estate road past Smugglers' Cove

☎ 450-0551
≈ 450-0281
www.splashresorts.com

Club St. Lucia's 369 rooms are spread out over its large landscaped property into separate cottage-style groupings or "mini villages." There are plenty of facilities for both adults and children. The standard rooms are clean, airy and functional. This hotel's real assets, however, are its two beachfront areas and its extensive watersports program.

Grande Anse

Bois D'Orange

Golden Arrow Inn
$110 bkfst incl.
⊗

P.O. Box 2037, Castries, 3.2km (2mi) north of Castries off the Castries Gros Islet Hwy.

☎ 450-1832
≈ 450-2459

The Golden Arrow Inn offers simple clean rooms with a balcony facing the water. A 3min walk takes you to a small private beach. Tough not outstanding, it is one of the most affordable hotels in this area.

The Orange Grove Hotel
$221

≡, ≈, ℜ

P.O. Box GM 702, Castries, follow the sign at Castries-Gros Islet Hwy. into Labrellotte Bay

☎*452-9040*

⇌*452-8094*

www.clubsinternational.com

Situated amid the hills of Bois D'Orange, the Orange Grove Hotel prides itself on providing patrons with personalized service in a unique setting. The rooms are relatively spacious, comfortable and pleasantly furnished with a view of Choc Bay from their balconies. There is a free shuttle to Choc Beach, where watersports equipment is available.

East Winds Inn
$853 all incl.

⊗, ≈, ℜ, ℝ, ◉

P.O. Box 1477, Castries, from the Castries-Gros Islet Hwy. take the road into Labrellotte Bay

☎*452-8212*

⇌*452-9941*

www.eastwinds.com

The long, rough road into the East Winds Inn creates an exciting air of seclusion as you enter this exclusive resort tucked unobtrusively into the corner of Labrellotte Bay. The beautiful grounds have been meticulously designed to teach visitors about St. Lucia's indigenous plants and birds. The circular cottage-style rooms with their palm frond canopies are unique, open, comfortable and fun, like a cozy treehouse.

Restaurants

The quality and variety of dining opportunities in Rodney Bay is exceptional, but prices will be expensive for long-term travellers on a budget.

Rodney Bay, Gros Islet and Pointe du Cap

Rodney Bay

Triangle Pub
$$

on the corner between the Rex Papillion and the Lime

☎*453-0224*

Tourists and Lucians alike enjoy the Triangle Pub's very reasonably priced grilled meats, salads and vegetarian platters. Its cafeteria-style-dining and large patio keeps things relaxed and unassuming. Between the live music nights and its location in the heart of Rodney Bay there's always a lively feel about the place.

Pizza Pizza
$$
across from Capone's restaurant
beside the Lime Bar
☎*452-8282*
Pizza Pizza serves casual,
no frills Italian food. It's not
a franchise operation, but a
simple sit down or take-out
restaurant frequented by
both Lucians and tourists.
Eat inside or out on the
patio by the water and children's playground.

The Cat's Whiskers
$$
closed Mon
north end of the Royal St. Lucian
☎*452-8880*
A spot for English ex-
patriates and anglophiles,
the Cat's Whiskers serves
standard English pub food
and ales. The atmosphere is
casual, friendly and on most
nights, full of animated
conversation fueled by a
few pints of good beer.

Snooty Agouti
$$
next to Pizza Pizza
☎*452-0321*
In an inviting treehouse-
style building, Snooty
Agouti is one of the most
unique restaurants in
St. Lucia. The atmosphere is
friendly, casual and relaxed
amid the funky wood de-
cor, local art and plenty of
open windows. An eclectic
menu of simple but tasty
fare is served accompanied
by an interesting selection
of cocktails and specialty

coffees. This is a great place
to read a book and escape
the heat or spend a rainy
day.

The Lime
$$$
across from the Rex Papillion hotel in
Rodney Bay
☎*452-0761*
Situated in the centre of
Reduit Beach, The Lime is
always a lively nightspot. A
moderately priced menu
featuring local ingredients
and traditional Creole
dishes is one of the main
reasons for this restaurant's
continued success.

Memories of Hong Kong
$$$
dinner only, closed Sun
across from the Royal St. Lucian
☎*452-8218*
The only Chinese restaurant
in Rodney Bay, Memories
of Hong Kong has been
serving Cantonese-style
dishes for years.

Capone's
$$$
closed Mon
across from the police station in
Rodney Bay
☎*452-0284*
Capone's Italian-style menu
covers all the basics like
pasta and pizza in tradi-
tional and not so traditional
ways. The dining area out
on the patio always has a
refreshing breeze and is a
good choice for a romantic
evening.

**Rodney Bay
and the North**

Rum Punch

A popular drink on cruises and at Lucian festivals, rum punch is the perfect sunset cocktail. It should be mixed in the following proportions:

One of sour: *lime juice*
Two of sweet: *sugar, syrup*
Three of smooth: *rum*
Four of weak: *nectar, juice and water*

Razmataz
$$$
dinner only, closed Thu
across from the Rex St. Lucian
☎452-9800

The only restaurant in St. Lucia serving authentic Indian tandoori cuisine prepared by a Nepalese chef, Razmataz is worth a visit as an interesting alternative to the standard fare offered around Rodney Bay. The lovely, airy interior and abundant greenery compliment the professional but unpretentious atmosphere.

Key Largo
$$$
East side of Castries-Gros Islet Hwy., north of Julians supermarket
☎452-0282

Fine traditional Italian cuisine served in a casual atmosphere is the essence of Key Largo's appeal. Pizza is prepared in a unique wood-fired oven and the range of pasta dishes goes well beyond the norm in terms of flavours and ingredients. There is also a children's menu and play area.

Spinnakers
$$$$
Reduit Beach beside the Royal St. Lucian
☎452-8491

Located on a quiet section of Reduit Beach, Spinnakers is a wonderful spot to enjoy a cocktail or a meal any time of day. Serving quality steak and seafood, this casual dining spot attracts both families and couples.

Half-Yellow Moon
$$$$
closed Tue
second street on the right after you enter Reduit, next to the Lime Bar
☎458-0565

Half-Yellow Moon's eclectic menu is mixed with an interesting selection of traditional Lucian foods. Regardless, the main attraction here is the romantic tropical ambiance of the roof-top garden and the quality live music featured nightly after 10pm.

Buzz
$$$$
closed Mon
facing the Royal St. Lucian
☎*458-0450*
Buzz, one of the newer establishments in Rodney Bay, bills its cuisine as San Francisco fusion. Owned by Pat Bowden, one of the most successful restaurateurs on the island, Buzz delivers professional service and an inspired menu with items like the salmon fillet with braised greens and a spicy coconut sauce.

Thai Royal
$$$$
Mon-Sat 5pm to 10:30pm
☎*452-9249*
second right off main Reduit road, back from the road on the right side
The elegant and authentic south Asian decor of Thai Royal provides a classy atmosphere in which to dine on spicy Thai dishes, such as *tom yam goong* soup or a curry like *gang ka ri*.

Eagles Inn
$$$$
end of main Reduit road past the Rainbow Hotel
☎*452-0650*
Situated at the northern tip of Reduit Peninsula, the Eagles Inn offers diners a unique view of Rodney Bay and the marina. The dining area, done in lovely wood trim, opens out to the water to take advantage of the refreshing seabreeze. The menu covers a broad range but the main focus is on seafood dishes prepared Creole style. Several berths are available for those who wish to sail in for their meal.

La Pergola
$$$$
breakfast and dinner
in the Marlin Quay hotel
☎*458-0598*
La Pergola's Mediterranean-style cuisine features vichyssoise, eggplant parmiggiano and chicken paso-doble. The seating is alfresco and the menu also includes cappuchino or espresso coffee and fine desserts.

Mortar and Pestle
$$$$
lower level of the Harmony Marina Suites Hotel, down the only street east of the Rex St. Lucian
☎*452-8711*
Dining at the Mortar and Pestle provides an opportunity to explore traditional dishes from across the Caribbean, like ginger pork St. Vincent, Guyana *casareep* pepper-pot stew and calaloo soup. Attentive service and lovely views of the marina in an outdoor dining area enhance the culinary experience.

Rodney Bay and the North

Charthouse
$$$$
dinner only, closed Sun
across from Thai Royal
☎*452-8115*
Beautiful decor, plenty of
wood trim and soft lighting,
give the Charthouse a warm
and inviting ambiance.
Diners are seated next to
the water and treated to
excellent service and a
hearty steak and seafood
menu. A selection of Cuban
cigars are also available for
an after dinner smoke.

Outer Rodney Bay

Coconut Willies
$
closed Thu
south end of the Marina Pl., second
level
☎*458-0506*
Overlooking the marina,
Coconut Willies is a small
open-air café serving drinks
and light lunches. A good
place to enjoy a sandwich,
take in the breeze and sip
rum punch.

Breadbasket
$
*Mon-Sat 7am to 6pm; Sun
7am to noon*
Rodney Bay Marina Pl.
☎*452-0647*
The Breadbasket is a popular breakfast spot for its
freshly brewed coffee,
French pastries and patio
by the marina. A selection
of tasty breads and sweets
is baked daily on the premises.

Burger Park
$$
closed Thu
beside the Castries-Gros Islet Hwy.
south of the Marina Pl.
☎*452-0811*
The Burger Park offers not
only burgers but also a mini
golf centre. There is a chil-
dren's menu and for adults,
an exciting selection of hot
and cold sandwiches such
as hot roast turkey with
avocado and grilled vegeta-
bles with basil oil on a fresh
baguette.

Three Amigos
$$$
south side of Rodney Bay Marina Pl.
☎*452-0351*
Three Amigos offers stan-
dard Mexican fare, including vegetarian burritos and
fajitas, at moderate prices. If
you have an overwhelming
craving for Tex-Mex food,
this is the only place in
St. Lucia where you have
any chance of satisfaction.
The other attraction here is
its location by the marina
and the private swimming
pool.

Bistro
$$$$
dinner only, closed Thu
west side of the Castries-Gros Islet
Hwy. just south of the Marina Pl.
☎*452-9494*
Much of the Bistro's appeal
is the attentive service,
quality cooking and dining
area on the water. The
menu consists mainly of
European and seafood
dishes. Yachties can moor

their boats at several berths adjacent to the restaurant. Reservations are recommended.

The French Restaurant
$$$$
dinner only, closed Tue
Castries-Gros Islet Hwy. south of the Marina Pl.
☎*450-0022*
Lucians and tourists come to the French Restaurant for authentic French Creole dishes, like salt fish *accras* and *lambi* soup. Patrons also enjoy the surroundings with its pleasant waterfront setting and trees towering above the patio.

Gros Islet

Budget travellers will appreciate the simple Creole dishes and reasonable prices in Gros Islet. There are a number of small restaurants around Dauphine and Marie Therese streets that are worth sampling for the food and the local atmosphere.

Everybody's Bakery
$
closed Sat
east side of Castries-Gros Islet Hwy. facing the Shell station
A rustic, white shack with blue doors, Everybody's Bakery sells tasty sweetcakes and fresh Creole loaves.

 Beaches
$$
Marie Therese St. south of Dauphine
☎*450-0714*
The friendly, laid-back ambiance of the Beaches explains why this is such a popular hangout with locals and travellers. What makes it even more special is its unique beachfront, where you can watch the sunset fade over Rodney Bay. The kitchen also serves simple but tasty Caribbean dishes like rotis, *accras* and curried chicken.

Pigeon Island

 The Captain's Cellar
$$
Mon 9am to 5pm; Tue-Sun 9am to midnight
Pigeon Island National Landmark, underneath the Interpretation Centre
☎*450-0253*
The unique setting of the Captain's Cellar in a historic 18th-century cellar draws people to this small café. After 5pm, there is free admission to the park so patrons have the beaches and beautiful park to themselves. The cozy ambiance, unique setting and well-prepared, mainly French, cuisine makes for a wonderful evening at a very reasonable price.

Rodney Bay and the North

🪵 Jambe de Bois
$$
south beach in Pigeon Island National Landmark
☎450-8166

The palm frond roof and hammock strung across the terrace should tell you that the Jambe de Bois is the kind of place to just hang out and savour the sensation of lying in a hammock on a Caribbean island. The menu is affordable and healthy with a very good selection of light breakfast food like fruit, muesli, yogurt and decent coffee. The water taxi from Rodney Bay to Pigeon Island drops you off at the dock in front of the restaurant.

Cap Estate

🪵 The Great House
$$$$
dinner only, closed Mon
west side of the main Cap Estate road, 2km (1.2km) north of Gros Islet
☎450-0450

An evening at The Great House is an exquisite dining experience. The theme of the restaurant lies in its illustrious past as the former estate of a French colonial official more than 300 years ago. The building's ornate facade, decor and period furniture set the tone. The sweet music of a baby grand piano could may well serenade you while you enjoy such dishes as roast duck breast with honey and balsamic vinegar or grilled

scallops with rosemary and olive oil. Seating is available on a terrace overlooking the ocean. Reservations are recommended and there is a dress code in effect (collared sports shirts are okay).

Cas en Bas

La Panache
$$$$
Wed dinner
2km (.5mi) down the Cas en Bas Rd., north side
☎450-0765

Once a week, La Panache guesthouse cooks up a traditional Creole meal for its guests and welcomes anybody else who's interested in a fun dinner event. You won't be disappointed with the fish, chicken or beef that's prepared using local ingredients and flavours. It's recommended you call ahead to reserve a space at the table.

Grande Anse

Bois D'Orange

Laurel's
$$
closed Sun
From Castries-Gros Islet Hwy. follow the turnoff for the Orange Grove Hotel, south side of the fork
☎452-8547

If you're out sightseeing and looking for a lunch spot off the tourist track, Laurel's is certainly worth a try. The menu is moderately priced and includes a good selection of home-style Creole dishes.

Entertainment

Rodney Bay

Half-Yellow Moon
closed Tue
second street on the right after you enter Reduit, next to the Lime Bar
☎*458-0565*
After 10pm the focus at Half-Yellow Moon is on live performances whether it be music, comedy or dance. Musical styles cover the entire spectrum from Latin jazz to reggae and blues. Every month there is a full moon party, while Wednesday is Latin vibes night and on Sunday, free salsa lessons are offered.

Happy Day Bar
north end of main Reduit road beside the Eagle Inn
☎*452-0650*
A tiny kiosk in a breezy waterfront location, the Happy Day Bar is sought out mainly for the unpretentious atmosphere and, of course, the two-for-one drinks all day.

Late Lime
Wed, Fri and Sat
across from the Papillion hotel beside the Lime restaurant
☎*452-0761*
The Late Lime's energized atmosphere and contemporary dance music consistently attracts a full house, made up of both tourists and locals.

Shamrock Pub
off the main Reduit road beside JQ Charles Mall
☎*452-8725*
Always a lively social spot, Shamrock Pub has pool tables, dart boards and a waterfront patio. Most nights of the week there's something happening: Tuesday is reggae night, Wednesday features the sounds of salsa, Thursday night karaoke is very popular, and Friday and Saturday are devoted to live music.

Snooty Agouti
next to Pizza Pizza
☎*452-0321*
Snooty Agouti serves great coffee and an impressive list of cocktails late into the night in a cozy, café atmosphere. Live jazz music is featured every Thursday, Saturday and Sunday night.

Triangle Pub
on the corner between the Rex Papillion and the Lime
☎*453-0224*
In the refreshing air of its patio, the Triangle Pub presents theme nights with

Rodney Bay
and the North

karaoke on Mondays, the live music of a steel band on Tuesdays, Creole jazz on Sundays, and a DJ on Friday and Saturday nights.

Outer Rodney Bay

Le Chalet
$10
Fri and Sat from 10pm
Castries-Gros Islet Hwy. south of the Marina Mall, above the French Restaurant
☎450-0022
Le Chalet is St. Lucia's only European-style club. Much smaller than Indies (see below), it is just as popular among both tourists and Lucians for its lively dance scene and waterfront location.

Indies
Wed: $39 women; $65 men; Fri and Sat $20
Wed, Fri and Sat
Castries-Gros Islet Hwy. just south of Julian's supermarket
☎452-0727
Indies is one of the most popular dance clubs in Rodney Bay. The music is loud and eclectic and the crowds are a mixture of young tourists and locals. On Wednesday nights, the entrance fee into the club's beach party (which takes place inside a large concrete nightclub) includes a ride to and from your hotel and drinks. A beach party it may be, but beachwear is prohibited.

Gros Islet

Friday Night Jump-up
Every Friday night, Gros Islet holds its famous jump-up, or street party, at the corner of Dauphine and Marie Therese streets. Open-air community socials have been a tradition in Caribbean life for centuries but this one is no longer just a local event, but a veritable tourist attraction. The cool, refreshing night air, much appreciated after a long day in the relentless heat, initially draws people out and creates the lively party vibe. On both sides of the street, vendor ladies form a line of coal-fired grills covered with spicy chicken and pots of hot oil frying dough, alongside a train of coolers full of beer. After sunset, the street teems with tourists, Lucians and blocks of speakers piled high and cranked loud to get everybody dancing. Expect a fun, friendly atmosphere but just to protect yourself against pickpockets or robbers take several precautions are advised: have a taxi drop you off and drive you home; bring only enough money for the night; stick to well-lit areas and avoid the beach and dark sidestreets.

Shopping

All the handicraft and souvenir shops are in Castries, but there are opportunities to purchase works by Lucian artists based in this region. **Zaka** *(next to Shamrock Pub,* ☎*452-0946)* in Rodney Bay sells unique Caribbean woodcarvings and masks. In Cap Estate, you can make appointments to view the beautiful silk prints of **Jean Baptiste** *(*☎*450-8000)* and the world-renowned prints and paintings of **Llewellyn Xavier** *(*☎*450-9155).*

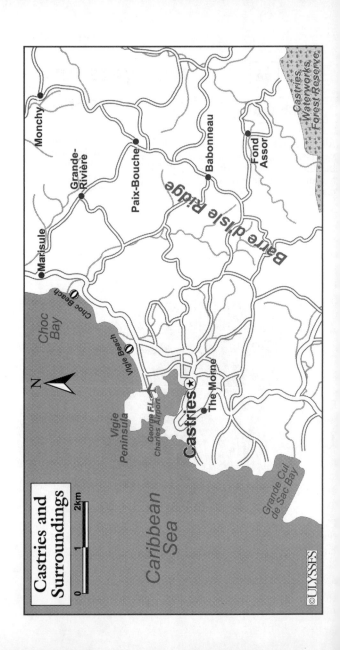

Castries and Surroundings

0 1 2km

N

Caribbean
Sea

Vigie
Peninsula

Choc Bay

Choc Beach

Vigie Beach

George F.L.
Charles Airport

Castries

The Morne

Grande Cul
de Sac Bay

Marisule

Grande-
Rivière

Paix-Bouche

Monchy

Babonneau

Fond
Assor

Barre dïsle Ridge

Castries
Waterworks
Forest Reserve

© ULYSSES

Castries and Surroundings

Imagine a British seaman at the bow of a four-masted battleship entering Castries ★ in the late 19th century.

The first thing he sees are the military fortifications surrounding the harbour. Less than a century before, France and England had fought their last battles over the island after 200 years of constant warfare. While this anxious sailor ponders his first night on dry land, Britain now fears the Americans, rather than the French.

On the left, portside, his ship passes the barracks, gun batteries and signal station of Vigie Point. To the right, starboard, La Toc Battery with its two powerful guns mounted on the hillside stands ever-vigilant, ready to strike enemy ships. Moving in closer, our sailor's commanding officer points to the top of the mountain that towers above

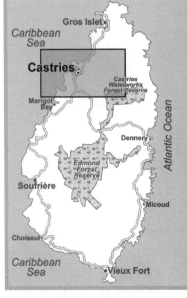

Castries at Morne Fortune, St. Lucia's military headquarters. There, faintly visible behind the Apostle Battery, a line of massive guns aims ominously down at the centre of the harbour. For two centuries, thousands of soldiers and rebels scrambled up the Morne's steep slope clutching a musket or machete before a hopeless battle or a surprise attack under the cover of night. French and British generals were well aware of the need to control this stronghold. If they gained control of Morne Fortune, they could control the island and one of its most important assets, the harbour.

Approaching by sea is an entirely fitting way to enter Castries. From the days of the first European presence on the island, Castries has been recognized as one of the finest harbours in the Caribbean. The high green mountains and hills surrounding the harbour shelter this large inlet from rough seas and inclement weather. Admirals and pirates were able to anchor their entire fleets here and still remain hidden from marauding enemy ships. Originally called Carenage, the French term for a boat landing, sailing ships came here for many years to have their hulls cleaned or repaired on the beaches. It wasn't until 1785 that this port was renamed by King Louis XVI in honour of his minister for the navy and colonies, the Marquis de Castries.

Drawing up to the warehouses and wharf of the town, this young sailor would certainly have noticed the governor's beautiful mansion perched conspicuously near the top of Morne Fortune. Once the symbol of British lordship over the colony, it is now the residence of St. Lucia's governor-general.

Flamboyant tree

A British seaman of the 19th century certainly wouldn't recognize Castries today. A modest enclave at the water's edge, it sprawls around the entire bay up to the top of the Morne. Over the centuries, Castries has been ravaged by a succession of fires and hurricanes. In 1948, the combination of a drowsy tailor, a burning candle and a strong seabreeze started the city's biggest fire, leaving more than 2,000 people homeless. Many important historic landmarks, like the post office and courthouse, were completely destroyed. As a result, the city is a mix of modern and colonial architecture. A bustling capital city of government buildings, restaurants and shops, more than a third of the island's population lives here. A telling sign of the times is the new multi-level parking lot in the downtown core, the first of its kind on the island.

For Lucians, Castries is the big city, with its crowded streets and scorching hot concrete, but there is also history, architecture,

shopping and fine dining to be enjoyed here. On the outskirts, you will find quiet places by the sea, in the forest or on a rocky bluff. But, most of all, amidst the urban scene, you will also find Lucian warmth and courtesy.

Finding Your Way Around

Castries is situated on the northwest coast of St. Lucia, between Rodney Bay and Soufrière. This chapter also explores the Cul de Sac Valley south of the city.

The great thing about Castries is that it is so compact that you can explore the entire city on foot. The downtown core is organized on a simple grid pattern of mostly one-way streets, so orienting yourself is fairly straightforward. Its also easy to get out of the city from the city centre. To head north take the John Compton Highway, which curves around the east end of the harbour before turning into the main Castries-Gros Islet Highway. The quickest way to head south is via La Toc Road and through the tunnel on the new highway. For excitement and impressive views, however, follow Bridge Street south over the top of the Morne. Both routes converge at the junction for Dennery and Soufrière.

By Air

George F.L. Charles Airport (☎452-1156) is located in Vigie, 5min north of downtown Castries, off the Castries-Gros Islet Highway. Smaller than Hewanorra in Vieux Fort, this airport handles mostly regional flights and local charter operators. If you land here, taxis can transport you to your hotel. The only other alternative, which is considerably less expensive, involves walking the length of the runway to the main road. From there, you can get a local minibus into Castries or to the north for less than $2.

Two helicopter companies offer island tours and shuttle services out of the airport.

Paradise Helicopters
☎450-9203
St. Lucia Helicopters
☎458-1390

By Car

The Castries-Gros Islet Highway is the main route into Castries from the north.

Coming from the south, follow the West Coast Highway which becomes the Morne Road and then leads into Castries. The other route is the new highway through La Toc which enters Castries on La Toc Road. It meets the West Coast Highway at the junction for Dennery by the Cul de Sac River.

Though finding a parking space downtown can be difficult, the recent opening of a multi-level parking lot north of the central market has greatly improved the situation. While driving downtown be sure to watch for one-way streets. Gas stations are located on Manoel Street and Chaussée Road, at the entrance to Pointe Seraphine on John Compton Highway and at the top of the Morne.

Car Rental Agencies

All the major car rental agencies are represented at George F. L. Charles Airport in Vigie.

A & A
☎452-1330
⇄458-1901

Avis
☎452-2046
⇄453-1536
Pointe Seraphine
☎452-2700
avisslu@candw.lc

Cool Breeze Jeep-Car Rental
☎458-2031

Hertz
☎451-7351
hertz@candw.lc

By Taxi

The main taxi stand in town
is located on the corner of
Jeremie and Coral streets.
By the entrance to the
Pointe Seraphine shopping
complex, you will not be
able to pass the taxi stand
without being asked in a
friendly, unaggresive way if
you need a cab.

A F Taxi
☎453-2492

A No.1 Taxi
☎453-1318

Always Ready Taxi
☎451-7966

Courtesy Taxi Co-op
☎452-1733

Finesse Night Taxi
☎453-1428

By Bus

Castries is full of commuters
so minibuses are available
to even the most out-of-
the-way communities.
St. Lucia's main mini-
bus terminal is located
downtown, east of the
Central Market. Stands for

the major routes to Gros
Islet, Soufrière and Vieux
Fort are all in this general
area. To find local routes or
to get a bus off the main
road, ask any of the drivers
to direct you.

Main bus routes:

No.1 *($1.50)*
Castries-Gros Islet

No.2 *($6)*
*Castries-Vieux Fort (via
Dennery)*

No.3 *($7)*
Castries-Soufrière

No.5F *($1.25)*
Castries-La Toc and the Morne

By Boat

The Inter-Island ferries dock
in downtown Castries is by
the jetty at La Carenage
Duty Free Centre. A ferry
(☎450-3595) runs every day
from 8am to 6pm between
here and Pointe Seraphine
Duty Free complex on the
other side of the harbour. A
one-way trip costs $3.

Green turtle

Practical Information

Tourist Information

St. Lucia Tourist Board
Mon-Fri 8am to 4pm and Sat 9am to 1pm
☎452-2479
The St. Lucia Tourist Board is located on the south side of Jeremie Street across from the police station.

Banks

Banking hours are Monday to Thursday 8am to 3pm and Friday 8am to 5pm.

Barclay's
ATM available
Bridge St. next to the post office
☎456-1125

Canadian Imperial Bank of Commerce
ATM available
William Peter Blvd.
☎456-2422

Caribbean Banking Corporation
Micoud St. across from Derek Walcott Sq.
☎452-2265

Royal Bank of Canada
ATM available
William Peter Blvd.
☎452-7855

Scotiabank
ATM available
William Peter Blvd.
☎456-2100

Mail

General Post Office
Mon-Fri 8:15am to 4:30pm
Bridge St. one block south of Jeremie St.

Post Restante

Post Restante letters are held at the General Post Office in a room at the back beside the National Development Bank Building. There is no charge for holding mail. Have your letters addressed as follows:

c/o Post Restante
Given Name, Family Name
General Post Office, Castries

Telecommunications

For overseas calls, faxes or telegram services, there is **Cable and Wireless** *(Mon-Fri 7:30am to 6:30pm and Sat 8am to 12:30pm; Bridge St. facing the post office;* ☎453-9000*)*. There are plenty of public phones in the downtown core, but the most reliable are lined up in front of Cable and Wireless.

Internet

Cable and Wireless offers Internet access at two loca-

ions and charges $5 for
30min. The service is available on the second floor of
the Bridge Street building
(Mon-Fri 8am to 4:30pm),
and at **Gablewoods Mall North**
near Choc Bay *(Mon-Fri
8am to 6:30pm)*. **PC Tech** *(70
Micoud St. at Chaussée Rd.;
☎453-6526; pceaglestar@
hotmail.com)* a computer
retailer, also offers Internet
services at $4 for 15min or
$10 for 1hr.

Pharmacies

R J Clarke
William Peter Blvd. and Bridge St.
☎452-2727

Fitz St. Rose Medical Centre
22 Micoud St.
☎452-3333

Marcellin's Pharmacy
1 Micoud St.
☎452-1473

Film

Cadet's One Diamond Photo Lab
Southwest corner of Hospital and
Manoel rds.
☎453-1446

Police

Police Headquarters
South end of Bridge St.
☎452-2854

Port of Castries
Jeremie and Bourbon Sts.
☎452-2372

Exploring

This chapter is divided into
three tours. **Tour A ★** explores the buildings and
attractions in downtown
Castries. **Tour B ★** brings
you to the outskirts of
Castries on the Vigie Peninsula. **Tour C ★★**, the lon-
gest of the tree, goes up
Morne Road and then south
into the interior to Barre
D'Isle Ridge.

Tour A:
Downtown Castries

This tour begins at the
Central Market ★★★ *(every
day 7am to 5pm)*, which is
located on the northeast
corner of Jeremie Street and
the John Compton High-
way. The market's original
steel structure opened in
1894 with a much less
distinguished extension
added in 1994. Inside,
vendors offer an assortment
of kitschy souvenirs and
local crafts, like wood
carvings, handmade
brooms, hot sauces, jewellery and batiks. The real
action, however, is outside,
at the east end of the market. Here, Lucians come to
socialize and buy or sell
their fresh fruit, vegetables,

meat and fish. There is also a string of small restaurant kiosks serving local food, which are very popular lunch and breakfast spots.

From the market's south entrance, cross Jeremie Street and follow Peynier Street into town. This area is at the eastern limit of the damage caused by the 1948 fire. After Constitution Park, on the right, is the latest reincarnation of the **courthouse**, a box-like structure made of sturdy, fire-resistent concrete.

One of the city's most prominent landmarks is the **Cathedral of the Immaculate Conception ★★** on Micoud Street. The size and location of this massive stone structure symbolizes the important role of the Roman Catholic Church in Lucian society. A church has occupied this site since the 1700s, but the current cathedral wasn't constructed until 1897. It's worth taking the time to wander inside and see how local artists have given the church a distinctive Lucian identity.

Across from the cathedral's clock tower, a giant 400-year-old saman tree shades the grass and park benches in **Derek Walcott Square ★**. It was the park's open space and the church's thick mortar walls that ultimately prevented the 1948 fire from advancing further east

or south. For over a century, this was known as Columbus Square, after that somewhat controversial figure in Caribbean history, and then in 1993 it was renamed in honour of St. Lucia's Nobel Prize winner for literature.

Overlooking the square, on Bourbon Street, is the **Central Library ★**. Constructed in 1925, with funding from the Carnegie Foundation, the building and most of its books were ravaged by the 1948 fire. In 1958, the library was restored and now a whole new generation of chatty high school students walks across its creaky wooden floors.

South of Derek Walcott Square, along **Brazil Street**, is one of the most picturesque street fronts on the island. A line of brightly painted balconies, gabled roofs, storm shutters and stylish wood trimming recreates an image of St. Lucia under colonial rule.

Follow Brazil Street east through an older section of town and make a right at Mary Ann Street. The small single-storey wooden homes squeezed into the narrowest of spaces are appropriately called **chattel homes**. Simply constructed and portable, they are a common sight in the Caribbean, where most people cannot afford to own prop-

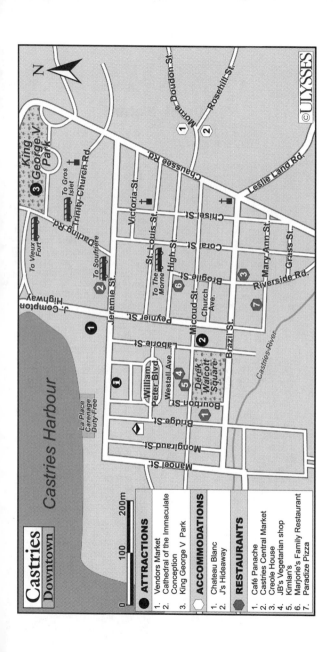

Castries
Downtown

Castries Harbour

La Place Carenage Duty-Free

J. Compton Highway

To Vieux Fort

To Soufrière

To Gros Islet

King George V Park

Darling Rd.

Trinity Church Rd.

Chaussee Rd.

Doudon St.

Rosehill St.

Morne

Leslie Land Rd.

Victoria St.

St-Louis St.

Chisel St.

Coral St.

High St.

Brogie St.

Mary Ann St.

Grass St.

Riverside Rd.

To The Morne

Micoud St.

Church Ave.

Brazil St.

Castries River

Jeremie St.

Peynier St.

Laborie St.

Westall Ave.

William Peter Blvd.

Bourbon St.

Derek Walcott Square

Bridge St.

Mongiraud St.

Manoel St.

0   100   200m

© ULYSSES

ATTRACTIONS
1. Vendors Market
2. Cathedral of the Immaculate Conception
3. King George V Park

ACCOMMODATIONS
1. Chateau Blanc
2. J's Hideaway

RESTAURANTS
1. Café Panache
2. Castries Central Market
3. Creole House
4. JB's Vegetarian shop
5. Kimlan's
6. Marjorie's Family Restaurant
7. Paradize Pizza

Derek Walcott

One of the Caribbean's most significant literary voices, Derek Walcott has earned international fame as both poet and playwright. Born January 23, 1930 in Castries, Walcott attended high school at St. Mary's College before attending the University of the West Indies in Jamaica. In 1953, he moved to Trinidad and became very active in the island's theatre community. Regional and international recognition began with the publication of his book of poetry, *In a Green Night,* in 1962, followed by the critically acclaimed play, *Dream on Monkey Mountain,* in 1967. In 1992, he was awarded the Nobel Prize for Literature, the second Lucian after Sir Arthur Lewis to receive such an award. Besides an illustrious and productive writing career, Walcott has also taught comparative literature at Yale and Columbia universities. He now lives in Trinidad and Boston.

In a region of evolving national identities, one of Walcott's greatest contributions is the power of his plays and poems to reveal West Indians not only to themselves but to the rest of the world. Critics often draw the connection between Walcott's mixed African and British heritage and his unique writing style, which fuses the structure of classical English literature with the vibrancy and creativity of West Indian dialects. Thematically, much of his work explores West Indian culture and the legacy of colonialism. Amid the tensions and conflicts inherited from colonialism, Walcott alludes to the struggle Caribbean societies face to preserve their Creole language and culture in an era increasingly dominated by British and American influences.

His most famous books of poetry are *The Castaway and Other Poems* (1965), the autobiographical *Another Life* (1973), *Sea Grapes* (1976), *The Fortunate Traveller* (1981), *Mid Summer* (1984) and *Omeros* (1990). His plays include *In a Fine Castle* (1970), *Remembrance* (1977) and more recently, a Broadway musical done in collaboration with singer Paul Simon entitled, *The Capeman* (1998).

erty. Think of them as the West Indian version of the trailer home.

After taking a left at Brogile Street, you'll arrive at the **Creole House** ★★ (see p 147) on the southeast corner of Brazil Street, another prime example of colonial architecture. Head upstairs and treat yourself a cold drink on the balcony—this is a rare opportunity to experience one of these beautiful old homes from the inside.

Follow Brazil Street past shops and a Methodist church, turn left and then continue 300m (1,000ft) north on Chaussée Road to **Holy Trinity Church** ★, on Trinity Church Road. Erected in 1842, with the stark presence of a medieval fortress, the church's highly visible location in this overwhelmingly Catholic nation was a source of great pride for its Anglican patrons.

A bit further up Chaussée Road, **George V Gardens** ★ *(free admisson; every day 24hrs)* offers a pleasant escape from the downtown heat and concrete with its tall, shady trees and flower gardens. Opened in 1893, two regal insignias adorn the west gates of this small park. Families promenade along its winding pathways, children play in the grassy fields and elderly people

chat on Victorian-style iron benches. The huge trees at the west end were probably original features when local community leaders created this park over a century ago. By the memorial in honour of the French Resistance is the botanical station, which has also been used by the Department of Forestry and the Red Cross. Its white turret is a classic example of flamboyant colonial architecture in the late 19th century.

If you would like a more in-depth look at the city, the **St. Lucia National Trust** *($26; contact Barbara, ☎452-1654)* runs an informative and enjoyable tour of Castries that highlights the city's architecture and history. The guided tour takes 1.5hrs and the fee includes an ice cream. A minimum of two people and at least 24hrs notice is required.

Tour B: Castries to Vigie Peninsula

Begin heading north on the John Compton Highway along the waterfront, past the Central Market and government buildings, through a section of town known as Conway. Once a small fishing village, it has been converted into the island's administrative centre. Around the bend, on the left, is the Fisheries Complex, where local fishers bring in their catch for cleaning and sale. Recently, Japan provided financial aid to upgrade the facility and strengthen the island's fishing industry. The Asian giant's interest in the Caribbean, however, goes beyond pure altruism. By co-opting small developing islands, like St. Lucia, with aid, Japan hopes to gain enough votes to overturn the current ban on commercial whaling.

The bold white pyramidal structure in the distance is the office of the **Alliance Francaise de Ste Lucie** *(Pointe Seraphine;* ☎*452-6468)*, an organization founded in 1954 to build cultural bridges between Lucians and the French.

When you reach the airport runway, turn right and at L'Anse Road make another right to the **Folk Research Centre** ★ *(donations accepted; Mon-Fri 8:30am to 4:30pm; P.O. Box 514, Castries,* ☎*453-1477)* 500m (1,600ft) ahead on the left. The centre is perched on a hill at the end of a long, shaded driveway in a re-stored colonial mansion. It was originally built in the early 1800s by P.J.K. Ferguson, a wealthy Scottish immigrant, to protect himself and his family from the constant outbreaks of malaria that plagued Castries at the time. This imposing stone residence, a curious mix of Georgian and Caribbean architectural styles, expresses Ferguson's nostalgia for the Scottish countryside. There is a wonderful view of Castries from the terrace and the small ramshackle rooms beside the house are former servants' quarters.

Opened in 1993, the Folk Research Centre is still in its infancy but the museum displays a small collection of cultural artifacts and traditional musical instruments. To really appreciate what the centre has to offer, however, its best to call ahead and request a tour. For a minimum of four people at $52 per person, you will be treated to rum punch, samples of local food and a folk dance demonstration accompanied by traditional instruments.

Continue north on the main highway, then left at the roundabout and left again along Peninsular Road beside the runway. Named in honour of one of the island's esteemed trade union leaders, **George F. L. Charles Airport** was opened in 1942, at the height of the Second World War.

After driving the length of Peninsular Road, you climb the short hill onto **Vigie Peninsula** ★★ and two former

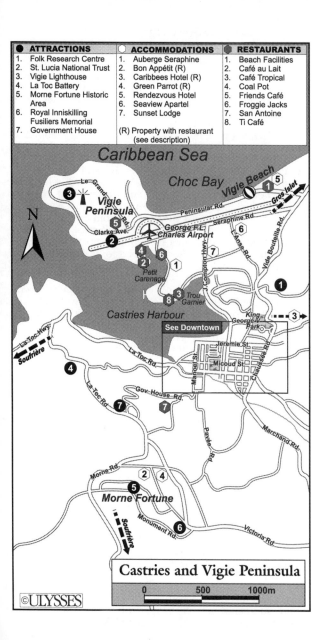

Caribbean Sea

Choc Bay

Vigie Beach

Le Grand Rd.

Vigie Peninsula

Peninsular Rd.

Seraphine Rd.

Gros Islet

Clarke Ave.

George F.L. Charles Airport

Vide Boutaille Rd.

N

J. Compton Hwy.

L'Anse Rd.

Petit Carenage

King George V Park

Trou Garnier

Castries Harbour

See Downtown

La Toc Hwy.

Soufrière

La Toc Rd.

Jeremie St.

Manoel St.

Jeremie St.

Micoud St.

Chaussee Rd.

La Toc Rd.

Gov. House Rd.

Pavée Rd.

Marchand Rd.

Morne Rd.

Morne Fortune

Monument Rd.

Victoria Rd.

Soufrière

Castries and Vigie Peninsula

0   500   1000m

©ULYSSES

colonial military barracks come into view, setting the tone for the rest of our tour. Until the French transferred their main fortifications up to the Morne in the 1740s, Vigie Heights was the most important stronghold in Castries. Today, these beautifully preserved landmarks house the French and Venezuelan embassies. Consider parking the car and walking the rest of the way. It's very pleasant to stroll along the shaded laneway that circles this affluent neighbourhood and historic area.

Follow Clarke Avenue straight ahead. On your left is the **St. Lucia National Trust** (see "Outdoors" p 78) and the National Archives. The thick tree canopy eventually opens up, revealing an **abandoned barracks**. A hollowed out skeleton of unshakable stone and mortar, the building sits on a slope facing Castries. A short distance below, in the flats of the airport runway, is the original site of Castries or, as it was known then, Le Petit Carenage. In 1767, the settlement was moved to its present location but this site remained an important military fortification.

To the left, a gravel road leads down into an underground stairwell, through an empty ammunitions hold, and then onto a concrete gun platform overlooking the water. Across

the bay is Taipon Rock, another former gun emplacement that now is occupied by a lonely ship's beacon.

Further along, Clarke Avenue winds around the hill past some of the most expensive real estate on the island. Tucked behind trees and tropical flower beds, a number of these homes date from the colonial period but most are modern constructions. Where the road forks, head left up to **Vigie Lighthouse** ★★, which was built in 1914. Like its namesake, Vigie has been used as an invaluable lookout station since 1722. Warnings of an approaching enemy naval fleet or a much anticipated merchant ship were relayed from this post to headquarters on Morne Fortune, but nowadays only a lighthouse operator is on duty. The panoramic view of Castries, the harbour and the blue expanse of the Caribbean Sea is splendid.

Retrace your steps to Clarke Avenue and at the next junction hang left onto Le Grande Road which brings you to **St. Mary's College**, a secondary school for boys run by the Roman Catholic Church. The school was moved into these old French military buildings in 1948 after its former downtown location was destroyed by fire.

At Clarke Avenue and Le Grande Road, continue east past the French embassy towards the airport. On your left is **Vigie Beach** ★★, a popular spot for locals who park their cars under the trees to cool off in the mid-day heat.

Tour C:
The Morne

This tour begins on La Toc Road, which is reached by taking Bridge Street south through downtown Castries, across the river, and turning right where the road forks along the waterfront. Across from the warehouses, freighters and the city's port facilities is Four a Chaux, an area once known for producing lime, the essential ingredient in mortar. For hundreds of years, this invaluable product obtained by heating sea shells fortified the colonial presence on the island in the sturdy foundations of estate homes, gun batteries and retaining walls.

La Toc Road curves sharply and then climbs a short distance up the west side of the Morne to **La Toc Battery** *(admission price varies according to the number of tour participants with a minimum of four; by appointment only and at least 24hrs notice;*

contact Alice Bagshaw ☎452-7921 or 452-6039). At La Toc, the Royal Engineers built an impressive battery of steel-reinforced concrete armed with two 18-ton guns capable of countering a sea attack. The battery was constructed in the early 1890s when Queen Victoria's British Empire was weary of the growing military strength of the United States. The presence of such a lethal artillery on the island compensated for the British fleet's absence while it was busy patrolling European waters because of increased German militarism. Although the guns were sold long ago, a tour of the fortifications takes you underground into the war shelter and tunnels where ammunition was stored. There is also an exhibit of old maps, gun shells and period artifacts.

Next, La Toc Road continues along the Morne's west shoulder behind Government House until it converges on Morne Road. Keep right around the top of the Morne, and at the gas station follow Henry Dulieu Road on the left into **Morne Fortune Historic Area** ★★★. In 1760, the French shifted their main fortifications in St. Lucia from Vigie Heights to Morne Fortune. From a military standpoint, the Morne is an ideal defense position which is why the

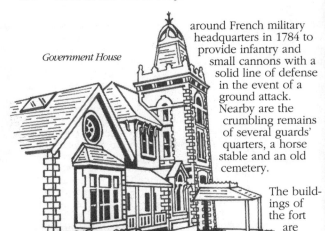

Government House

around French military headquarters in 1784 to provide infantry and small cannons with a solid line of defense in the event of a ground attack. Nearby are the crumbling remains of several guards' quarters, a horse stable and an old cemetery.

The buildings of the fort are now occupied by **Sir Arthur Lewis Community College**. A stroll through the old barracks and offices is like a trip back in time. Most are well preserved and accessible to the public, but bear in mind that classes may be in progress. Indeed, the .5m (2ft) mortar walls were built to withstand artillery attacks and also to keep the interiors cool in the tropical heat. On any given day a century ago, a British commander could have shut the thick metal door of his office and walked along the arched verandah, stroking his waxed mustache with a baton tucked under his arm, and then descended the iron stairwell, imported from foundries in England, to the Officer's Mess for tea and a puff of his pipe.

British maintained a fort here when the French lost the island for the last time in 1814. The British named it Fort Charlotte and continued to fortify this stronghold until it was finally abandoned in 1905. The government is currently in the process of restoring the area.

On your left is **Apostle Battery.** Built by the British in 1888, it strengthened the island's defense system with four huge guns powerful enough to hit targets 1,100m (3,600ft) away. A short distance up the road is **Prevost Redoubt**, the only example of French earthworks left untouched by British construction crews at the turn of the 19th century. This is one of five earth and mortar redoubts built

At the southeast corner of Fort Charlotte, near the tomb of Sir Arthur Lewis, St. Lucia's Nobel Laureate for Economics, is the **Royal Inniskilling Fusiliers Memorial**. Unveiled by a certain Captain H.M. Know in 1932, it stands as a memorial to soldiers of the Inniskilling Regiment, who defended the Morne against a French attack in 1796. The monument is a minor point of interest, however, compared to the outstanding panoramic view of the entire island. Looking to the north from this breezy plateau, Gros Islet is clearly visible next to the signal station on top of Pigeon Island. Facing south, Mount Gimie and the two Pitons mark Soufrière on the distant western coastline.

Back on the Morne Road, the tour descends the south face of the Morne into the Cul de Sac valley. At the junction, follow a winding road east through banana plantations towards Dennery and the Atlantic coast. After the village of Bexon, the curves sharpen as you ascend the heights of Barre de L'Isle Ridge, which divides the island into east and west. At the top of the pass, on the right-hand side, is the trailhead for **Barre D'Isle Ridge Trail ★★★** (see p 139). This hike takes you along the ridge through the jungle and up to the top of Mount La Combe.

On your return to Castries, follow the Morne Road north until it meets Victoria Road and becomes Government House Road. Originally built in 1895, picturesque **Government House ★** was the former residence of British governors and is now home to St. Lucia's governor-general. Unfortunately, the house is not open to the public. There is, however, a brilliant view of the city by the roadside in front of the residence. After a steep descent down a series of exciting switchbacks, the road enters Castries on Manoel Road.

Beaches

Vigie Beach

This is a pleasant beach that gets even better further north of the airport. It's a lovely walk in the surf north to Vide Bouteille Point. There is excellent swimming along the way and several restaurants and bars for food and refreshments.

Outdoor Activities

Cruises

One of the island's most interesting day cruises is aboard the Brig Unicorn. Its big claim to fame is a feature role in the film *Roots*. Here is an opportunity to experience the thrill of sailing in a tall ship and to also see how crews a century ago would have sailed these waters. The tour costs $210 and leaves Castries from the dock west of the Pointe Seraphine duty-free complex. The boat stops in Soufrière for several hours to visit local attractions.

Brig Unicorn
☎*452-6811*

Deep-Sea Fishing

All the big game fish, like blue marlin, tuna and kingfish, are found in the open waters off the coast of Castries. Two experienced charter outfits, based in Vigie Marina, offer beginners as well as seasoned

anglers half- or full-day charters.

Hackshaw Boat Charters
☎*453-0553*

Captain Mike's Sport Fishing and Pleasure Cruises
☎*452-7044*

Helicopter Tours

Two tours are available: a 10min tour of the northern tip of the island from Pointe Seraphine to Pigeon Island and the Atlantic Coast, and a 20min south island tour to Soufrière and over the rain forest. You can also charter helicopters for aerial photography and longer flights around the entire island.

Paradise Helicopters
☎*450-9203*

St. Lucia Helicopters
☎*458-1390*

Golf

Sandals
$78 one round
every day 8am to 4pm
☎*452-3081*
Sandals at La Toc Bay operates a nine-hole public golf course.

Hiking

Barre D'Isle Ridge Trail

Barre d'Isle Ridge
$25 including guide
Mon-Fri 9am to 4pm
☎*450-2231*
This trail offers an exciting hike along the top of Barre d'Isle Ridge, which divides the island into east and west. The fee for this hike is paid at the forestry office across the road from the trailhead. You can park your car either there or on the shoulder of the road, which is quite wide.

In the past, this trail was an old footpath used by Caribs, brigands, soldiers and peasants to travel across the more rugged areas of the island. The first section of the trail starts out in a beautiful pine plantation and then leads you into a dense tropical forest. Along the way, you'll see massive chatagnier trees, several scenic look-out points and perhaps hear parrots chattering in the jungle canopy. The other half of the trail is a steep climb up to the summit of Morne La Combe. This section is the most demanding and not recommended for young children or the seriously unfit. At the top is a won-

derful view of Grand Rivière in the middle of the Cul de Sac Valley, Dennery on the coast and the mountains surrounding Mount Gimie.

Scuba Diving

Dive Fair Helen
☎*450-1640*
From their base in Vigie Marina, Dive Fair Helen can bring you to dive sites in the north, such as Labrellotte Bay, or in the south to Soufrière Marine Management Reserve. Night dives, equipment rental and instruction are also available.

Sailing

Castries is an official Port of Entry for Immigration, but the sailing literature recommends clearing customs in Rodney Bay or Marigot Bay to save time. When you enter Castries, you must go directly to the Customs Dock. There are anchorages at Pointe Seraphine (☎452-3036) and Vigie Marina (☎452-5057 or VHF 16) with repair services and restaurants. For other supplies, downtown Castries is only a short distance away. If

you're interested in chartering a sailboat try **Douglas
Sailing Tours** (☎457-7777).

Submarine Cruises

There are hour-long underwater cruises that let you
explore coral reefs and
sunken ships. Trips depart
seven times daily from the
dock at Pointe Seraphine.

Sadko Submarine
☎453-6201

Whale-Watching

During a half-day tour,
odds are excellent that you
will encounter one of the
many species of whales and
dolphins in St. Lucia's waters. Hackshaw Charters has
hydrophones so you can
listen in on whale conversa-
tions under the water.
Operators are based in
Vigie Marina.

Hackshaw Boat Charters
☎453-0553

**Captain Mike's Sport Fishing
and Pleasure Cruises**
☎452-7044

Accommodations

Downtown Castries

 **Chateau Blanc
Guesthouse**
$67
⊗, *sb*
Morne Doudon Rd., east of Chaussée
Rd.
☎452-1851
Located in a lovely colonial-
style home in a relatively
quiet section of the downtown area, Chateau Blanc is
one of the best deals on the
island for budget travellers.
The rooms are simply fur-
nished and very clean.
Guests stay on the upper
level with its wood floors,
reminiscent of an earlier era
in the Caribbean, and
wooden shuttered windows
overlooking the street or
the backyard. There is also
an airy common area under
a covered terrace and a
fully equipped shared
kitchen.

J's Hideaway Guesthouse
$70
⊗, *sb*
Morne Doudon Rd., east of Chaussée
Rd.
☎451-9521
Clean and affordable, J's
guesthouse is located minutes from downtown. Meals
and drinks are available

upon request. The main draw here is the price and location.

Caribbees Hotel
$221
≡, ≈, ⊛, ℜ, ℝ
P.O. Box 1860, top of La Pansée Rd.
☎*452-4767*
≈*453-1999*

Situated on a hill in the midst of a quiet residential area, one of the most striking features of the Caribbees Hotel is its breathtaking view of the city. Very comfortable and tastefully furnished in rattan, these rooms also come with private balcony or patio and include all the conveniences, like a blow dryer, iron and ironing board. This is a favourite of business travellers who enjoy its conference facilities, quiet atmosphere and two fine restaurants.

Castries to
Vigie Peninsula

North of Castries

Sunset Lodge
$104
≡, ℜ
John Compton Hwy., facing Pointe Seraphine
☎*452-2639*

Sunset Lodge offers clean and functional rooms near the airport, Vigie Beach and downtown Castries. The service is warm and personal but the highway traffic is noisy.

Seaview Apartel
$125
≡, ⊗, ℜ, *K*
P.O. Box 527, corner L'Anse Rd. and Castries-Gros Islet Hwy.
☎*452-4359*
≈*451-6690*

Situated 5min from the airport and Vigie Beach, Seaview Apartel is appreciated by business travellers for its location, modern facilities and professional staff. The rooms are well furnished and comfortable, with plenty of open space in the kitchen and sitting area. They also have balconies facing the sea.

Vigie Peninsula

Auberge Seraphine
$239
≡, ≈, ℜ
P.O. Box 390, Castries, Pointe Seraphine Rd. at Vigie Marina
☎*453-2073*
≈*451-7001*

Located in the quiet surroundings of Vigie Cove, Auberge Seraphine caters mainly to business travellers and airline pilots. Staff has a friendly but thoroughly professional attitude. All the rooms are comfortably furnished with a balcony overlooking the water and the local Cattle Egret colony. If you want to relax by the sea, there is a free shuttle to Vigie Beach.

Vigie Beach

Edgewater Beach Club
$156

≡, ℜ, ℝ, K

P.O. Box 962, Castries, 500m north of airport on Castries-Gros Islet Hwy.

☎/⇄452-4872

Located on Vigie Beach, the Edgewater Beach Club offers clean and simple motel-style accommodations. Guests will appreciate the intimate service and privacy of a smaller hotel, which sets it apart from the resort scene. Kitchenettes and spacious rooms also provide independence and a money saving option for families.

Rendezvous Hotel
$525

≡, ≈, ⊛, ℜ, ☺

P.O. Box 190, Castries, follow airport entrance road past Vigie Runway to the right of the cemetery

☎452-4211
⇄452-7419

The Rendezvous is an all-inclusive hotel for couples only. The emphasis here is on romance and relaxation. On the grounds of an impressively landscaped beach front property, guests have access to all the amenities and sports activities of an international resort chain.

Choc Bay

Sundale Guesthouse
$91

⊗

behind south end of Gablewoods Mall N., access from first road south of the mall

☎452-2410

The Sundale Guesthouse is the most affordable accommodation in this area. Though the grounds are uninspiring, the rooms are simple, clean and guests have access to a common kitchen. Choc Beach is only a short walk away.

Beach Walk Inn
$106

⊗, ℝ

P.O. Box 464, Castries, east side of Castries-Gros Islet Hwy. facing Choc Bay

☎452-2523
⇄453-7812

For the money, Beach Walk Inn offers the best accommodation in this area. The standard rooms are small and modestly furnished but clean and come with a balcony overlooking Choc Bay. Its only a 5min walk to Choc Beach where watersports facilities can be rented at Waves Restaurant and Bar.

The Morne

Bon Appétit
$96 bkfst incl.
⊗, ℜ
P.O. Box 884, Castries, Red Tape Lane
50m south of the Green Parrot
☎452-2757
The four standard rooms at Bon Appétit share wonderful views from the top of Morne Fortune. The fair-size rooms are adequately furnished and offer travellers reasonable accommodation for the price. A friendly and conscientious staff add a personal touch to the service and keep the atmosphere pleasantly casual.

Green Parrot
$200 bkfst incl.
≡, ≈, ℜ
P.O. Box 648, Castries, corner Victoria Rd. and Red Tape Lane on the Morne
☎452-3399
⇰453-2272
Perched on the Morne overlooking Castries, the Green Parrot offers views from your balcony that take in the entire harbour, Gros Islet and, on clear days, Martinique. This is one of the older hotels in Castries, which explains the retro-style furnishings and the wild mustangs oil print at the reception. All the rooms are modestly comfortable, open and spacious with high ceilings and large sliding glass doors to the balcony which let in plenty

of natural light. Be fore-warned: there are lots of stairs on the premises.

Restaurants

Downtown Castries

J B's Veg Shop
$
Mon-Sat 7am to 5pm
Westall St. between William Peter Blvd. and Micoud St.
One of the many street vendors catering to the lunch crowd in the downtown area, JB's serves healthy, inexpensive vegetarian food. The menu is limited to several dishes including rice and peas, dal and cold drinks, but it's prepared daily and always tasty. Cash only.

Castries Central Market
$
every day 6am to 5pm
A strip of vendors on the east side of the market serve simple inexpensive Creole fare like fried chicken, rotis, fish and egg sandwiches, soups, hot drinks and vegetarian platters. Meals are sit down or take away but you might want to stay for awhile and watch the buzz of activity in the market. Cash only.

Kimlan's
$$
closed Sun
22 Micoud St. opposite Derek Walcott Sq.
☎**452-1136**

One great reason for stopping at Kimlan's is the balcony and the chance to watch the street action below around beautiful Derek Walcott Square. It is often crowded with Lucians who come here for reasonably priced meals (meat or vegetarian) and snacks. The English breakfast is recommended for budget travellers.

Café Panache
$$
closed Sun
Bourbon St. facing Derek Walcott Sq.
☎**453-1199**

Patrons of Café Panache will find a good selection of simple American, Creole and French fast food and snacks like baguette sandwiches and roti. The cafeteria-style service explains why prices are so reasonable, while the stylish decor gives it a classy atmosphere.

Paradize Pizza
$$
Mary Ann St. between Peynier and Brogile Sts.
☎**451-7999**

Fast affordable pizza and other Italian dishes are served at Paradize Pizza. Don't let the lacklustre decor turn you off because the pizza's good, the vibe is pure local and cold beer is available.

Marjories Family Restaurant
$$
25 High St. between Peynier and Brogile Sts.
☎**452-7295**

Always busy at noontime with hungry office workers, Marjorie's Family Restaurant delivers fine, home-style Creole dishes. In addition to rotis, vegetarian plates and fresh local juices, there is stewed beef, lamb or chicken.

Garden City
$$$$
top of La Pansée Rd. in the Caribbees Hotel
☎**452-4267**

Perched atop La Pansée Hill, Garden City offers fine dining in an open setting dominated by a stunning view of Castries. The menu features a good selection of Creole food, such as cream of pumpkin soup, but also caters to European tastes. Considering the location and first-class service, prices are very reasonable.

Castries to
Vigie Peninsula

Ti Café
$
Mon-Fri 8am to 5pm; Sat 9am to 2pm
the kiosk west of the information centre at Pointe Seraphine duty-free

Strategically located in the path of disembarking cruise

ship passengers, the Ti Café serves light pastries, sandwiches and specialty coffees, including locally grown coffee.

Café Tropical
$
Mon-Fri 8am to 5pm; Sat 9am to 2pm
northeast of the information centre at Pointe Seraphine duty-free
☎452-7411
The ice cream counter at Café Tropical is a popular spot for shoppers looking for a place to sit down and cool off. A selection of light snacks and lunch dishes is also available. The small bar, on the other side of the building, sells cocktails and beer.

Friends Café
$$
Mon-Thu 8am to 5pm; Fri and Sat 8am to midnight
Vigie Heights, corner Le Grand and Clarke aves., below the Venezuelan Embassy
☎458-1335
After a walk around Vigie, Friends Café makes a great breakfast or lunch spot. Staff from the two embassies and offices nearby come here for the freshly ground coffee, rotis and the very good selection of pastries. Situated on the ground level of a historic military building, the café offers both indoor and outdoor seating.

Café au Lait
$$
Mon-Fri 8am to 7pm, Sat 8am to 4pm, Sun 8am to 3pm
south side of Vigie Marina beside the Coal Pot
☎453-0959
In the early morning or midday heat, Café au Lait is a wonderful place to relax in the cool breeze next to the water. This unassuming patisserie serves continental breakfast, sandwiches and scrumptious desserts as well as fine ice cream and coffee.

Waves
$$
Castries-Gros Islet Hwy. at Choc Beach, 200m (600ft) south of Babonneau junction
☎451-3000
Locals and tourists from nearby hotels come to Waves for the affordable Creole buffet, drinks on the beach and its laid-back, casual atmosphere. Its other attraction are the beach toys for rent.

D's
$$$
closed Sun
in the Edgewater Beach Club on Vigie Beach, Castries-Gros Islet Hwy. 500m (1600ft) north of the airport
☎453-7931
D's eclectic menu of American, European and Creole dishes will appeal to a wide range of tastes. This small beachfront restaurant offers good meals and a refreshing seabreeze on a shel-

tered patio. Several vegetarian meals and soups are available.

Froggie Jack's
$$$$
closed Sun
Pointe Seraphine Rd. in Vigie Marina
☎*458-1900*
The interesting blend of French and Creole dishes on the menu at Froggie Jack's is one reason why this is such a popular restaurant—the other being the quiet garden atmosphere on the dining terrace overlooking Vigie Marina and the marvelous view of Morne Fortune. To enhance the experience, you can take a water taxi or ferry here from Castries.

Coal Pot
$$$$
Mon-Sat noon to 2pm, 7pm to close
south side of Vigie Marina
☎*452-5566*
An award-winning restaurant, the Coal Pot offers patrons exquisite fine dining in an intimate atmosphere. A small number of tables are set on the wooden terrace next to the water. Creole and European cuisine are featured along with a selection of fish plates like kingfish, dorado, and swordfish, served in various sauces including wild mushroom or coconut curry. Accessible by water taxi or ferry.

The Morne

Bon Appétit
$$$$
dinner only from 7pm
Red Tape Lane 50m (160ft) south of the Green Parrot
☎*452-2757*
The unassuming ambiance and spectacular view from the top of Morne Fortune gives Bon Appétit its special appeal. Having only a few tables gives the setting a special intimacy and ensures that patrons receive personalized service. House specialties include freshwater crayfish, steak and fresh hearts of palm.

The Green Parrot
$$$$
corner Red Tape Lane and Victoria Rd.
☎*452-3399*
Established 28 years ago, the Green Parrot serves Continental cuisine alongside unique Creole dishes like Fish St. Lucie Colbert. In an elegant upscale environment, patrons can sit either indoors, amidst the colonial-style furniture and antique fixtures, or out on the breezy terrace with a sweeping view of Castries and the northern coastline.

San Antoine
$$$$
closed Sun
Old Morne Rd., E. of fork at Government House Rd.
☎*452-4660*
Housed in a late-19th-century hotel, San Antoine is

considered one of the best restaurants in the Caribbean. The refined ambiance and elegant decor set the tone for an upscale menu of Creole and European specialties like butterfly shrimp Creole and escalope of veal with caper butter. All this and a beautiful view of the harbour. Reservations are recommended.

Entertainment

Downtown Castries

Creole House
closed Sun lunch
southeast corner Peynier and Brogile Sts.
☎*452-3238*
Located in the heart of downtown Castries, on the second floor of a lovely old colonial building, Creole House is both a mellow afternoon stop and a lively night spot. In the evening, a younger Lucian crowd moves in and the island music pumped out of a loud sound system provides a fitting soundtrack for people watching from the balcony.

Castries to Vigie Peninsula

Beach Facilities
closed Sun
Vigie Beach, 25m (80ft) left of Rendezvous Hotel
☎*452-5494*
Beach Facilities is the place where Lucians and tourists come to relax at the south end of Vigie Beach. The shaded patio and cool seabreeze make Beach Facilities an ideal place to sip cocktails, watch the sunset or escape the midday heat.

Friends Café
Mon-Thu 8am to 5pm; Fri and Sat 8am to midnight
Vigie Heights, corner Clarke and Le Grand aves., below the Venezuelan Embassy
☎*458-1335*
Friends Café serves alcoholic drinks in a warm and interesting atmosphere. Saturday night features games like darts, dominoes and backgammon. Come for a cold drink and take a seat after a walk along Vigie Beach or up to the lighthouse.

Waves
Mon, Tue, Thu, Sat, Sun 8am to 7pm; Wed, Fri 8am to 11pm
Castries-Gros Islet Highway at Choc Beach where the road bends sharply inland
☎*451-3000*
Located at the south end of Choc Beach, Waves attracts

tourists and locals for beer and cocktails by the water some Friday nights. Live music is featured.

Shopping

Castries is one of the best areas on the island for shopping. At **Pointe Seraphine Duty-Free Shopping Complex** and **La Carenage Duty-Free Centre** *(both Mon-Fri 9am to 5pm, Sat 9am to 2pm and, if a cruise ship is in port, Sun 9am to 4pm)* you will find many international boutiques like Benetton, Colombian Emeralds and shops selling Lucian art. Across from the Central Market is the **Vendors Market** *(every day 9am to 5pm)* where you will find everything from local crafts and cigarette papers, to sunglasses, T-shirts and hats. Downtown along Micoud and High streets, Rastas sometimes have stands set up with interesting organic jewellery, hats, handicrafts and the usual assortment of

smoking supplies. For the best selection of books, newspapers and magazines on the island, there is **Sunshine Bookshop** *(☎452-3222)* at the corner of Jeremie and Laborie streets.

On the Morne, **Caribelle Batik** *(☎452-3785)* is worth a visit for the silk-screen workshops, lovely batik clothing and a stroll through the lovely garden of a century-old Victorian home. **Eudovic's Art Studio** *(☎452-2747)*, on the south slope of Morne Fortune, showcases this acclaimed woodcarver's art and visitors can watch some of his apprentices at work. The **Modern Art Gallery** *(☎452-9079)* exhibits contemporary Lucian and Caribbean art. One of the oldest exhibition spaces on the island is the **Artsibit Gallery** *(☎452-7865)* at the corner of Brazil and Mongiraud streets. **Gablewoods Mall North** in Choc Bay, has several duty-free stores, a supermarket, Internet access and the **Sunshine Bookshop**. Another supermarket is **JQ's** on William Peter Blvd.

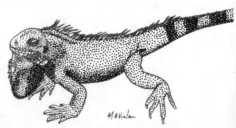

Soufrière and the West Coast

One of the most dramatic views in the Caribbean unfolds in Soufrière and the West Coast ★★★ during the 540m (1,800ft) descent into Soufrière from Columbette.

The panorama of mountains, forests and the Caribbean Sea appears suddenly, like a final crescendo, after the exciting drive along the island's spectacular southwest coast. The Pitons, St. Lucia's most famous landmarks, tower above Soufrière and the fishing boats in the harbour. Across the valley, whiffs of sulphuric steam rise from the smoldering remains of Qualibou, a collapsed volcano. You might even be lucky enough to see the tall ship *Brig Unicorn* sail gracefully into Soufrière Bay.

In the southwest, St. Lucia's Creole language and culture remains strong, with atois com-

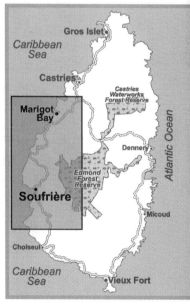

monly spoken in Fond St. Jacques and the villages surrounding Canaries and Anse La Raye. Farmers cook "one pot stew" on traditional coal pot stoves while they tend their crops. In downtown Soufrière, many excellent examples of Creole architecture still exist, in spite of a massive fire that swept through the north end of town in 1955. Creole baguettes are baked daily and the majority of restaurants serve Creole-style cuisine.

The southwest is also recognized as the island's ecotourism centre. Outdoor enthusiasts will find many different activities for exploring this beautiful region. Hike through the rain forest in one of several large forest reserves, enjoy a refreshing swim under waterfalls in Canaries and Anse La Raye or ride horseback through a restored colonial plantation. There are whale-watching tours and scuba divers can choose from one of many protected dive sites in the Soufrière Marine Management Reserve.

Traditional coal pot stove

The quality and style of accommodations in the southwest is unsurpassed on the island. Amid the beautiful scenery are a number of unique hotels celebrating not only the region's natural surroundings, but also its history and culture. Mago Estate Hotel is brilliantly designed with a cozy treetop nook and restaurant built into a cliff. Guests at working plantations, like historic Fond Doux Estate and The Still Plantation, learn about Lucian history, how the land was settled and how it is cultivated today. There is wonderful dining at luxurious Anse Chastanet Resort and stunning views of the Pitons from the rooms at Ladera Resort or the Jalousie Hilton.

This chapter explores the rugged mountainous region along the Caribbean coast from Gros Piton in the south to Marigot Bay in the

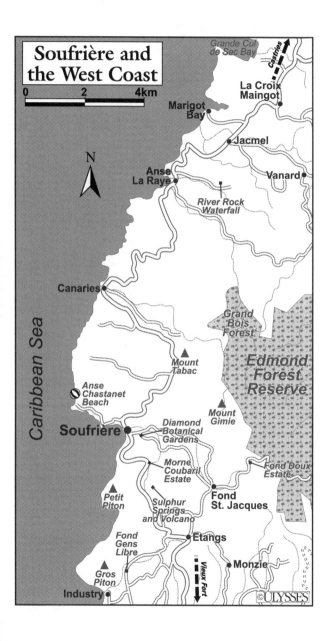

"Don't mind the Joneses" - Soufrière graffiti

north. It features three tours. **Tour A** ★★, introduces you to Soufrière and the beautiful valley of Fond St. Jacques and the island's precious rain forest.

Tour B ★★★, winds along the West Coast Highway through the fishing villages of Canaries and Anse La Raye and a major banana growing area to Marigot Bay, a cove for sailboats and swimming.

Tour C ★★★, heads south through historic plantations and the exciting geography of the Pitons.

Finding Your Way Around

From Castries or Vieux Fort the West Coast Highway will bring you to the town of Soufrière. It's the only road along the coast so travelling around the south-west on your own is easy. Should you decide to explore one of the secondary roads into the interior, don't be too apprehensive about getting lost. They lead to dead ends or loop back to the main road after a scenic drive through the countryside. If you do manage to get lost, just ask a local.

By Car

Driving around the sharp curves, hairpin turns and steep hills that are typical of this mountainous region is exciting in itself. There are plenty of places to explore off the main road that do not necessarily require a four-wheel-drive vehicle. Make a point of using your horn to warn oncoming traffic, just as Lucian drivers do. In the higher elevation forest areas, watch for the deep rain gutters on both sides of the road. Gas stations are located in Anse La Raye, Canaries and Soufrière.

Car Rental Agencies

Soufrière

Cool Breeze Car and Jeep Rentals
☎*459-7729*
☎*459-5017 (Jalousie Hilton)*

CC Rentals
☎*459-5771*

Marigot Bay

Charlery's Car Rental
☎451-4645

By Bus

Minibuses run regularly
between Castries and
Soufrière along the coastal
highway. They operate
every day, but service is
slower on Sundays. Drivers
only leave when the van is
full so departures are more
frequent during peak com-
muter hours, especially on
routes to and from Castries.

Minibus Routes:

No. 3 *($7)*
Castries–Soufrière

No. 4 *($8)*
Soufrière–Vieux Fort

By Boat

Water taxis are available in
Soufrière and will take you
anywhere on the coast even
as far north as Pigeon Point.
Fares are set according to a
fixed government rate.

Soufrière Water Taxi
☎459-7239 or 459-7990

By Taxi

Soufrière Taxi Association
☎459-5562

South Western Taxi Association
☎459-5740

Scott Taxi and Tour
☎459-7463

Practical Information

Tourist Information

St. Lucia Tourist Board
*Mon-Fri 8am to noon, 1pm to
4pm and Sat 8am to noon*
Bay St., by the harbour, opposite the
Texaco station
☎459-7419
Friendly staff provide you
with travel information,
maps and an air condi-
tioned refuge.

Banks

Barclays
ATM available
Bridge St. south of Sir Darnley St.
☎459-7255

National Commercial Bank
opposite Barclay's on Bridge St.
☎459-7450

Post Office

corner of Bay St. and Sir Darnley
Alexander St. by the jetty

Telecommunications

Outside of your hotel, public phones are available by the post office in Soufrière and in central locations in smaller communities.

Photography

There are no photography shops in this region, but hotels and dry goods stores have film available. In Soufrière, look in **Chez Camilla's Fast Food Restaurant** (☎459-5379) on Bridge Street; sometimes they sell film.

Supermarkets

In Soufrière, all the major supermarkets *(Mon-Thu 8am to 8pm, Fri and Sat 8am to 9pm, Sun and holidays 8am to 1pm)* are located around the town square by the Catholic church. Allains closes on Wednesdays at 12:30pm.

Police

corner Bay St. and Sir Darnley Alexander St.
☎459-5646

Exploring

Tour A:
Soufrière to
Fond St. Jacques

This tour begins in picturesque **Soufrière ★★★**, the largest town in the southwest. Because of a major fire that destroyed much of the north end of town in 1955, Soufrière is divided architecturally into old and new sections. Fortunately, some of the older buildings were spared. The old section of town is dominated by the steeple of the **Catholic church** and the town square bordered by Princess and Sir Arthur Lewis streets. In this area, brightly coloured colonial-style homes with balconies and wooden shutters line the streets. The north end of town, called the New Development, consists of less stylish concrete buildings, like the town hall and police station.

The tour heads east out of Soufrière up the valley of Fond St. Jacques on Sir Arthur Lewis Street. After a short distance the road

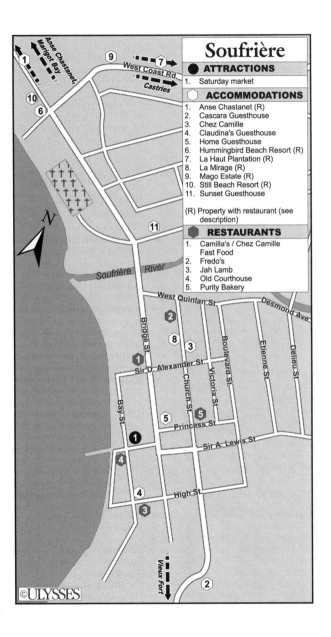

Soufrière

● ATTRACTIONS

1. Saturday market

◊ ACCOMMODATIONS

1. Anse Chastanet (R)
2. Cascara Guesthouse
3. Chez Camille
4. Claudina's Guesthouse
5. Home Guesthouse
6. Hummingbird Beach Resort (R)
7. La Haut Plantation (R)
8. La Mirage (R)
9. Mago Estate (R)
10. Still Beach Resort (R)
11. Sunset Guesthouse

(R) Property with restaurant (see description)

⬡ RESTAURANTS

1. Camilla's / Chez Camille Fast Food
2. Fredo's
3. Jah Lamb
4. Old Courthouse
5. Purity Bakery

Anse Chastanet / Marigot Bay

West Coast Rd.

Castries

Soufrière River

West Quinlan St.

Desmond Ave.

Bridge St.

Sir D. Alexander St.

Bay St.

Church St.

Victoria St.

Boulevard St.

Etienne St.

Delieu St.

Princess St.

Sir A. Lewis St.

High St.

Vieux Fort

©ULYSSES

passes historic **Soufrière Estate**, on the right, one of the original estates in this area. Like the entrance to an English manor or a French château, the long, tree-lined driveway to the main house disappears behind a tall wire fence into a lush green forest. Neither the driveway nor the building is open to the public.

In 1713, King Louis XIV of France was anxious to settle St. Lucia so land was made available to his subjects. Many arrived from other islands in the West Indies, particularly Martinique, where arable land had become scarce. Large-scale European settlement began in Soufrière when three brothers from the Devaux family received an 800ha (2,000-acre) land grant in honour of their services to the crown. By 1743, the forest had been cleared and a plantation was growing crops like cotton, indigo and tobacco. Later, the fields were turned over to sugar cane and, when that was no longer profitable, citrus fruits and cocoa.

The estate is still owned by descendants of the original Devaux family (which includes the DuBoulays) and now operates mainly as a tourist attraction. Although many of the plantation buildings were destroyed by the big hurricane of 1780 and during the Brigand War (see p 28) which took place on the island in the aftermath of the French Revolution, some, like the restored sugar mill and water wheel, remain.

At the first right, follow the sign to the **Diamond Botanical Gardens, Mineral Baths and Waterfall** ★★ *($7 for gardens, $7 for public bath, $10 for private bath, $15 nature trail, gardens and waterfall; Mon-Sat 10am to 5pm, Sun*

Soufrière Catholic church

and holidays 10am to 3pm; ☎459-7565) which is the latest incarnation of Soufrière Estate. In 1784, an analysis of the estate's spring water by the Medecins du Roi in Paris revealed that it was very similar to other famous medicinal baths in Europe, like Aix la Chapelle in Germany and Aix les Bains in France. Soon after, a number of baths were built on the estate at the behest of King Louis XVI for his troops in St. Lucia. The original baths were abandoned after being destroyed during the Brigand Wars. It wasn't until 1930, when Andre DuBoulay restored two of the baths for his own use, that any attempt was made to recover them from the forest.

In the middle of a small gorge surrounded by lovely tropical flowers and plants, visitors can bathe in newly constructed public and private baths. In the distance is the sound of Diamond Waterfall streaming down over a wall of rock brightly coloured by the minerals in the water. The baths are not actually fed by the waterfall, but by an underground source which originates at Qualibou volcano. It's a wonderfully relaxing experience, and if you opt for the private baths, ask the attendant to point out the original stone baths nearby.

Adjacent to the mineral baths, Diamond Botanical Gardens contains an impressive collection of indigenous plants and flowers. On the grounds of a former cocoa and citrus plantation, a path leads you through this beautifully landscaped garden. It's a pleasant place for a walk and perfect for a picnic on one of the shaded benches. You can continue further on a recently built nature trail through the forest to see the restored sugar mill and gigantic water wheel.

Returning to Sir Arthur Lewis Street, turn right and follow it across the Soufrière River, continuing right up the valley on what is now Fond St. Jacques Road. Below the road, the tail end of the Soufrière River flows into a wide plain before arching west into the sea. Many early settlers, like the Devaux family, did not penetrate much further inland from the coastal areas. Normally, they stayed close to the sea, not only because it offered security, accessibility and transportation, but because such areas are particularly fertile and the flat terrain allowed for large-scale farming.

Opposite the bus shelter in Zenon is the **New Jerusalem Warm Waterfall** ★ *($5; every day 8:30am to 6pm)*. A path leads from the road down to a footbridge across the

Bamboo

Bamboo is a common sight in the higher elevations of the southern part of St. Lucia. It grows naturally in clumps in tropical climates, in wet and cool conditions. A member of the grass family, some species of bamboo can grow to 40m (130ft) and 30cm (12in) in diameter. Although it has the size and appearance of a tree, bamboo grows as quickly as grass. In fact, it grows faster than any other tree and can be harvested every three to five years.

Bamboo is a crucial link in any ecosystem for a number of reasons. It absorbs huge quantities of water, preventing soil erosion on steep slopes and holding the soil in place during the rainy season which, in turn, reduces the possibility of a landslide disaster.

In many parts of the world, bamboo is an indispensable building resource. For its weight, it is one of the strongest materials on earth. It is often used to reinforce concrete floors on construction sites. While more commonly associated with furniture, in the tropics bamboo is used for houses, aqueducts and fences. In Asia, the young shoots are eaten as a vegetable.

river and then up a short hill to the gardens and waterfall, or more precisely, the showers. Visitors shower under spring water, ranging in temperature from hot to cold, surrounded by lush tropical vegetation. Sticks of bamboo channel an underground water source into a concrete basin which is scrubbed daily. Most of the fun, however, is just getting to the showers and exploring the vicinity. A changing room and toilet are available.

Tucked into a ravine by the next bridge is **La Toraille Waterfall** ★ (*$5; every day 9:30am to 5:30pm*), where you can cool off in a pool fed by a 15m (50ft) waterfall. After a landslide destroyed much of the property in February 2000, the garden was replanted with a lovely array of exotic and native flowers like ginger lily, bird of paradise and wax candle. Higher up the slope, overlooking the garden, you can dry off in the sun with a view of Petit Piton. Families with small children will appreciate the short distance around the garden and the shallow pool. You can purchase alcoholic and non-alcoholic drinks at the entrance and there are changing rooms and toilets.

About 1,000m (3,200ft) ahead, yet another waterfall awaits you in the village of Ravine Claire. Before you decide that all waterfalls look alike, bear this in mind: half the fun is getting there. This is definitely the case at **Spyke Waterfall** ★ ★ ($5; *every day 9am to 5pm*), which not only offers a great hike, but a spot to cool off at the end!

To enter, approach the booth by the roadside; if it's empty, go to the house next door. The trail to the waterfall leads up the ravine and climbs up a fairly steep slope through the forest. Steps have been built into the path to make the climb easier and to provide better footing in the rainy season.

The climax comes when the tree canopy breaks and you walk onto a rocky bulge into the middle of Spyke Waterfall, which is actually a series of small cascades stretching 105m (350ft) over exposed rock and boulders. From this point, there is a wonderful view of Fond St. Jacques and, a bit further down, there is a place to cool off in the stream. The route back to the trailhead passes small country homes surrounded by chickens and pigs. You will also find an abandoned sugar-cane press once powered by the river and a coffee grinder still in use. Drinks are available from the bar next door.

In St. Phillip, the next village to the east, you begin to see the valley narrow into a deep fold along the riverbed. The tall slopes rise higher and steeper, hemming in the homes that line the valley floor. At the bus shelter, keep left past the Catholic church and the elementary school. After you cross Migny River, the smooth asphalt deteriorates quickly into potholes and bumps. In this environment, maintaining a smooth surface is next to impossible, with huge amounts of rain streaming down the hillsides, eating away at the road's thin layer of stone and pavement. Homes and crops in this area are also extremely vulnerable to

Soufrière and the West Coast

being crushed in a landslide. The danger has increased in the last decade because farmers have been clearing the forest on some of the valley's upper slopes. This ultimately weakens the soil's foundation during the rainy season when the exposed soil becomes saturated with water and simply gives way under the enormous weight.

When prices were high in the 1970s and 80s, many farmers in this area planted bananas, but now most have changed over to dasheen for sale to hotels or at the central market in Castries. This tuberous plant covers most slopes in the valley with its big green leaves shaped like an elephant's ears. It is an ideal plant for this type of climate since it absorbs large amounts of water. It's a local tradition for young farmers starting out on their own to plant citrus trees like grapefruit and orange as a kind of retirement fund.

During the last set of switchbacks up to the top of the pass, the quaint wooden homes disappear

and you are left alone to enjoy the lush scenery and wonderful views of the valley. Rounding the bend at the very top you feel a strong blast of fresh air that blows across the rain forest from the Atlantic Ocean. The road on the left leads to Deroche and some lovely views of Fond St. Jacques and the Caribbean Sea. For an adventure off the beaten track, you can climb **Morne Gimie ★★★**, St. Lucia's tallest peak at 936m (3,118ft).

Our route follows the road to the right along the valley's southern edge. Every day farmers walk up the steep road from their homes lower down in the valley to tend their dasheen plantations on the fertile hills of this area. It's difficult work, but after nine months the rich volcanic soil provides bountiful harvests. When they mature, the dasheen are dug up, pruned of their upper leaves and then put in large sacks for market. In most cases, transporting the produce involves carrying a 50kg (110lb) sack on your shoulders up a long steep slippery hill to the roadside

Old sugar-cane press

fishing boats and nets are common sights on this island and provide the perfect subjects for photographers! - Chris Higgins

Excited schoolchildren in uniform arrive at this school in Soufrière. Many of St. Lucia's schools were founded by the Catholic Church.

- *Chris Higgins*

The setting sun illuminates the town of Soufrière, which is dominated by the Pitons, St. Lucia's most famous landmarks.
- *Chris Higgins*

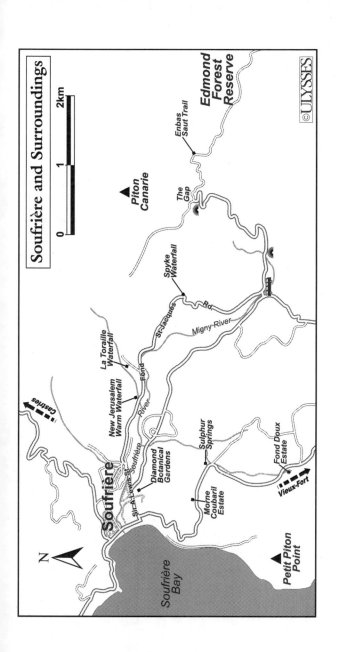

The rough road passes Piton Canarie and winds east to the **Enbas Saut Waterfall Trail** ★★★ (see p 171). A path of bright red earth leads visitors through virgin rain forest in the Central Forest Reserve to see the spectacular Enbas Saut Waterfall. The road eventually comes to a dead end at the entrance to the **Edmond Forest Reserve** ★★★ (see p 172) which covers much of the southeastern region of the rain forest.

On your return to Soufrière from the end of Fond St. Jacques Road, turn left by the bus shelter where the road forks. On the other side of Soufrière River, you can either follow the paved road to Bois D'Inde and the West Coast Road or turn right on the old inland road to Fond St. Jacques into the village of Espérance. In the latter case, after passing several small wooden homes, turn left where the road climbs steeply for a great view of Mount Gimie and the valley, which gives you a vivid sense of the region's geography. Eventually, this road meets up with the paved highway in Bois D'Inde. Make a right at the West Coast Road and follow it past Fond Doux Estate to Soufrière.

Tour B: Marigot Bay

This tour follows Bridge Street north out of Soufrière, climbing the long road up the ridge. At the north end of Soufrière Bay is a small beach area used mainly by hotel guests as an alternative to the swimming pool. The water is calm and the sand is maintained regularly. Further along, at the north end of Bridge Street along the north side of the the bay towards Rachette Point, is **Anse Chastanet Beach** ★★★. This is the best beach in the area, with fine sand and a bar nearby (see p 170).

Returning to Bridge Street, turn left and make your way up the north ridge above Soufrière. At the top is a **lookout platform** with a marvelous view of town and the valley of Fond St. Jacques, Mount Gimie and the Edmond Forest Reserve in the distance. The road continues inland around the base of Mount Tabac on the right, then as you near the sea coast again, along the top of Ravine Duval past bamboo and tree ferns. Between January and March, amid the abundant greenery of breadfruit and mango trees, the route is enlivened by the bright orange blossoms of the immortelle tree.

It wasn't until 1959 that a surfaced road was built into **Canaries ★**, an event that fundamentally changed life in this small fishing village. Although the first wave of French settlers reached this area in the early 18th century, it could only be accessed by boat or a rough dirt track. When the sugar industry collapsed on the island, estates in Canaries turned to bananas for survival. Unfortunately, crops were so badly damaged by the bumpy roads that many plantations went bankrupt.

Just before you cross the bridge into Canaries, take the road on the right down to a wide dirt track. An hourlong hike alongside the Canaries River takes you to a series of beautiful **waterfalls** deep in the forest. When you return, reward yourself with food and drinks, available at several restaurants in town.

Bananas

Along a short stretch of highway north of Canaries, in Anse La Verdure, you can purchase fresh cassava bread from vendors on the west side of the road. Cassava is made from the manioc plant and was a staple for indigenous peoples and slaves. The highway continues weaving in and out of ravines around Mount Parasol before descending to sea level at **Anse La Raye ★★**. Originally named by sailors for the rayfish that gathered in the cove, the town's beach is lined with fishing boats and its streets dominated by a Catholic church built in 1907. At the north end of town, on the right, a sign directs you to **Anse La Raye Waterfall** which is reached after a short drive and hike into the forest.

Not long after Anse La Raye, the first road on your left brings you to a secluded beach cove, covered with fine, honey-coloured sand, called **Trou L'Oranger ★★** (see p 170). Continuing north, the highway veers west towards the sea with the steep mountains receding to the interior and the dense vegetation thinning to pockets

Rastafari

At the height of its popularity in the 1970s and 80s, the reggae music of inspired singers like Peter Tosh, Bob Marley, Burning Spear and Culture introduced Rastafarians to the world. Today, the popular image of a dreadlocked Rastafari has become synonymous with the Caribbean. It's an ironic twist, considering that they were for many years viewed as outcasts by Jamaican society and, in the very early days, even demonized.

The term Rastafari comes from to Haile Selassie, the former emperor of Ethiopia, who called himself Ras Tafari: "ras," a prefix in Amharic, the Ethiopian language, means an aristocrat, comparable to the English term duke, while "Tafari" refers to the name of his family. When he assumed the throne in 1930, Jamaican mystics interpreted the arrival of this new African king as the coming of a black messiah, as prophesied by Revelations 19 in the New Testament. They worshipped Haile Selassie as a divine being and formed the first Rastafarian groups. The regal images of this black emperor are coveted by Rastafarians as a symbol of their faith and a source of inspiration for realizing their own potential.

What it actually means to be Rastafarian is hard to define. On a philosophical level, Rastafarian beliefs are rooted in the teachings of Marcus Garvey who, at the turn of the 20th century, led the movement for black repatriation to Africa. Garvey's political activities eventually forced him into exile from Jamaica, but his ideas about black self-reliance and cultural pride continued to attract followers. Rastafarian values embody a deep reaction against a society dominated by white political and religious institutions. The system is considered "Babylon," a source of oppression and evil for its inequalities, materialism and disharmony with nature. Instead, Rastafarians look to African symbols, styles of dress, chanting and drumming to gain a sense of cultural identity that was stolen from black people during the time of slavery.

Many of the forms and symbols associated with Rastafarians are the products of African and Asian influences in Jamaican society. The wearing of long dreadlocks is the most obvious, with the length of one's "dreads" being a source of pride, since it is a measurement of time spent as a Rastafarian. There is also the belief, rooted in African and East Indian cultures, that to cut one's hair is an affront to God because the act denies our natural selves. Thirty-five years ago, dreadlocks were an oddity; now they are a fashion trend. The wearing of dreads is no longer a reliable indication of a true Rastafarian. In reference to this fact, Bob Marley once said "there are many wolves in sheep's clothing."

Originally introduced to Jamaicans by East Indian labourers, marijuana is considered a sacrament by Rastafarians. In their eyes, God or "Jah" created this plant, like all other natural things, for the use and benefit of humans. Smoking the herb is a form of meditation and a source of divine guidance. For good health and moral reasons, devout Rastas only eat "Ital" which is a strictly vegetarian saltless diet. African slaves in Jamaica associated the eating of salt with a weakened spiritual state.

In the 1930s and 40s, Jamaica and the rest of the Caribbean experienced severe social and economic problems as a result of extreme unemployment and poor living conditions. By the 1950s, Jamaicans saw little improvement in the situation. Thousands of poor peasants had migrated from the country to the cities looking for work, only to find themselves stuck in urban poverty. A feeling of severe disaffection took hold of many younger Jamaicans and it was at this time that Rastafarians became a more common sight on the streets of Kingston and in the countryside. Although it took longer for the movement to reach the smaller islands of the Eastern Caribbean, conditions were similar enough to those in Jamaica that it quickly gained popularity.

Today, Rastafarians are accepted and respected and have joined the mainstream of Caribbean society. Not only are there Rastafarian musicians and artists, but lawyers, politicians and successful business people. There are white and black Rastas in the UK, Canada, the United States, Europe and Africa. In some Caribbean countries, including St. Lucia, they have organized themselves into political parties.

of brown grass and short trees.

A sheltered platform overlooks **Roseau Valley**, a wide flat basin of banana trees flanked by low-lying hills. This land was covered in sugar cane until the early 1960s when Geest Industries, a large Dutch food exporter, bought the entire estate to plant bananas for the lucrative UK market. Geest still plays an important role in St. Lucia's banana industry, but Roseau has since been subdivided and sold to small farmers.

The highway heads north in a long straight line across the valley floor. For decades, bananas have sustained St. Lucia's economy, providing farmers with an important source of regular income. Driving through the plantations, you will see the sheds where the bananas are sorted, dipped in herbicide and then packaged. Farming practices are extremely labour intensive here, one of the major disadvantages Lucian farmers have against their competitors in Central America. The World Trade Organization's decision in the late 1990s to uphold the elimination of British subsidies to banana farmers in the former colonies has made it even harder for these operations to make a profit. If you have a minute, stop and look around; don't be afraid to ask farmers a question—they're friendly and always happy to promote their product.

At the first major junction, a left turn brings you to the **Roseau Rum Distillery ★** *($13; Mon-Fri 9am to 3pm; ☎451-4315)*. A lighthearted and fun tour of the distillery is available that includes a short lesson on the history of rum.

Back on the main highway, make a left at the next junction to get to the picturesque cove of **Marigot Bay ★★**. This may be one of the most famous places in St. Lucia to swim and sunbathe, but due to its location, hotel guests and yachties are its only visitors. Surrounded by rocky bluffs with a narrow sandbar topped with coconut palms across its middle, Marigot is very much an idyllic setting. Hollywood felt the same way and featured it in the movie *Dr. Doolittle*.

This is also a popular spot among yachting enthusiasts, who come from all over the world to overnight in St. Lucia's famous harbour. There is a ferry to the north side of the bay *($2; every day 24 hrs/day)*. If you would like to spend some more time here, there are a number of fine hotels and restaurants around the bay as well as a small beach that's great for swimming. To return to Soufrière, retrace your route to the junction at the main highway and turn right.

★★★

Tour C:
Gros Piton

Our tour begins at the town square in front of the Catholic church and heads south on Church Street out of town where it becomes West Coast Road. The road quickly climbs up a ridge where there is a viewing platform, before it continues further down the coast. From the lookout, Mount Tabac rises in the northeast above Soufrière, and Rachette Point, on the far side of the bay, reaches out to the sea. In November 1999, Sea Storm Lenny destroyed many homes and boats on Soufrière's south shore along Baron Drive. Throughout the ordeal there was no rain or strong wind, just three days of rising water that ultimately swallowed up the shoreline.

Further along the highway, on your right, is the unmistakable **Petit Piton**, a gigantic volcanic rock formation soaring to a height of 738m (2,461ft). The Caribs worshipped this rock, which they called Attabera, the goddess of fertility, moving water and tides.

As you round the Piton's northeast face, turn right at the Jalousie Hilton sign onto Jalousie Road, an

Soufrière and the West Coast

indestructible strip of concrete that guarantees visitors access to the resort whatever the weather. Keep left at the fork until you reach the **Pitons Warm Waterfall** ★ *($5; every day 8am to 6:30pm)*. Comfortably seated in the middle of a tropical forest, you can bathe in warm mineral water from a nearby spring to the tranquil sound of a small waterfall.

Opposite Jalousie Road, on the main road, is **Morne Coubaril Estate** ★★ *($15; Mon-Sat 9am to 5pm, Sun 9am to 3pm, ☎459-7340)*. From a charming estate house to meager slave huts, the buildings on this estate have been preserved or rebuilt to show visitors how a plantation would have looked a century ago. There is also an opportunity to watch crops like cocoa and coconut being processed using traditional methods. Hiking trails run throughout this beautiful property or you can also arrange for an exciting tour on horseback.

Further south on West Coast Road, across from the bus shelter, is St. Lucia's much publicized **Sulphur Springs and Volcano** ★ *($3; every day 9am to 5pm; ☎459-7686)*. In pre-Columbian times the indigenous peoples in this area called it Qualibou, or "the Place of Death." French settlers called it a *soufrière* and geologists refer to it as a "coldera." Formed approximately 50,000 years ago, it's not actually a bubbling cauldron but the remnant of a collapsed volcano that once spewed enough lava to create much of this region. The volcanic steam you see is escaping through vents or small lesions in the crater surface. Visitors were permitted to walk on the crater until one fateful day when, during a demonstration, a tour guide accidentally stuck his foot through one such hole hidden underneath a pile of loose ash, seriously burning himself.

In the 1830s and 40s, sulphur was mined from the crater for export. More recently, efforts were also made to harness the steam as a source of power for the island, but enthusiasm and funding dwindled so now the leftover machinery sits idle in an overgrown patch of grass.

Lucians claim soaking in the warm sulphurous streams near the crater is good for arthritis and rheumatism. The unpleasant odour you'll notice is hydrogen sulphide gas which is not dangerous.

The tour continues south along West Coast Road to **Fond Doux Estate** ★★ *($10; tour with lunch $40; Mon-Sat 9am to 4pm; ☎459-7545)*. Established during the initial wave of French settlement in the early 18th century, Fond Doux is one of the oldest estates on the island. In 1795, brigand units fought off a British force here at the Battle of Rabot, and as a result, maintained control over this part of the island.

When sugar prices dropped at the end of the 19th century, many plantations in this area switched to cocoa and coffee and later added citrus fruits and bananas. The estate is still very much in the business of producing cocoa, and exports most of its crop to Hershey's in the United States. In the fresh mountain air, organized tours explore the history and natural beauty of the estate and include demonstrations of how cocoa is processed. You can also hike on your own through the scenic countryside on a network of trails leading to the famous battle site or to the forest, past citrus groves, an abandoned sugar mill and century-old immortelle trees.

The tour heads further south on West Coast Road through some of the most fertile soil on the island. Hundreds of thousands of years ago, when Qualibou was a tall, young, erupting volcano, it spewed layer upon layer of volcanic mud, boulders and ash over this area and eventually created

the giant slope down to the sea that dominates the terrain. This soil, rich with nutrients and minerals, is responsible for the lush, densely covered landscape. Coconuts are a common crop and used to make copra, one of St. Lucia's biggest exports. Copra is the white meat of the coconut, which is dried and pressed into an oil used in soaps, cooking oil and body lotions.

Turn off the highway at the next right onto an unpaved road towards Union Vale. Keep right until you reach the village of **Fond Gens Libre** on the other side of L'Ivrogne River at the base of the impressive **Gros Piton** ★★★ 786m (2,619ft). Towering above them, it is not surprising that Caribs worshipped this gigantic pillar of rock. They called it Yokahu, the powerful god of volcanic mountains, sun, fire, thunder and food. St. Lucia is currently trying to have the Pitons designated as a Unesco World Heritage Site.

During the 18th and 19th centuries, groups of escaped slaves and brigands took refuge in this area, hence the name Fond Gens Libre meaning "Village of the Free People." Gros Piton provided a fortress and watchtower for defense against their enemies. Perched on a round gray boulder, hidden behind a thick blanket of green foliage, brigand soldiers would scan the coastline from points around the Piton looking for British troops approaching from Soufrière or Vieux Fort. Near the base on a small plateau, they set up camps where they slept with their fires low and dim, under gigantic boulders or in caves tucked away from sight in the forest.

A signpost will lead you to the trailhead for the **Gros Piton Nature Trail ★★★** (see p 173). In the last few years, the local community of Fond Gens Libre and the St. Lucia National Trust combined efforts to build this trail. They have done a marvelous job of exposing visitors to Gros Piton's natural features as well as its historical and cultural importance as a brigand stronghold (see p 28).

Instead of returning to Soufrière along the same route, turn right at West Coast Road, and at the next major junction make a left and then another quick left to Belfond Drive. The asphalt is broken and bumpy but travelling slowly gives you the opportunity to enjoy the wonderful view of Qualibou, Fond St. Jacques and the

Quilesse Forest Reserve to the northeast. The road loops back to the main highway; turn right to get to Soufrière.

Beaches

★★★

Anse Chastanet

Aside from great swimming and wonderful scenery at Anse Chastanet Beach, the reef beyond the dock offers fantastic snorkelling. All the equipment you need can be rented from the hotel's dive shop. If you feel like getting away from the hotel, it's also possible to explore the shoreline further north to another small beach known as **Anse Mamin**.

★★

Trou L'Oranger

Nestled between high rocky bluffs, at the end of a dirt track north of Anse La Raye, Trou L'Oranger is ideal for swimming, exploring and romantic picnics.

Dolphin

Outdoor Activities

Cycling

**Jungle Biking Adventures
☎451-2453**
Jungle Biking Adventures at Anse Chastanet resort operates an exciting network of mountain bike trails through the forest and the historic buildings on a former plantation. The trails are designed for a wide range of skill levels and the $127 fee includes a bike, helmet and water bottle.

Deep-Sea Fishing

Half- and full-day fishing charters can be arranged at the office of the **Soufrière Marine Management Area** (☎459-5500).

Hiking

Plenty of hiking can be done on roads and tracks around Soufrière, particu-

larly in Fond St. Jacques (see map of Soufrière and surroundings p 161). There are also walks to waterfalls on public land in Anse La Raye and Canaries.

Mount Gimie

The trail up to the top of St. Lucia's highest mountain starts at the end of Deroche Road and leads through secluded dasheen plantations, across rivers and finally into a misty rain forest before arriving at the most demanding section of the climb near the summit. On clear days, there is a splendid panorama of the island. A guide can be hired at the **Department of Forestry** (☎450-2231). If you have the time, it's well worth the trek.

Enbas Saut Waterfall Trail

This trek begins on a narrow ridge winding around tall stands of bamboo and over the roots of big trees like the chatagnier and bois de canon. In the shadow of Piton Canaries and Piton Troumassée, parrots and smaller birds such as the St. Lucia oriole, mountain whistler and the St. Lucia black finch flitter about the forest canopy in large numbers. After a steep climb down the slope of the valley, you reach the headwa-

Soufrière and the West Coast

ters of the Troumassée River, which eventually drains into the Atlantic Ocean south of Micoud.

One of the most striking waterfalls on the island, Enbas Saut drops about 18m (60ft) into a pool deep enough for bathing. Above the waterfall, there is a short side trail that merits a closer look. The way back involves a hard, unrelenting climb up the side of the valley, which is why this hike is not recommended for the terribly unfit or young children. There is a changing area by the falls so bring along a bathing suit. For information and a guide contact the **Department of Forestry** *($25 with a guide;* ☎*450-2231).*

Edmond Forest Reserve

The trail in this section of the reserve is much less demanding than Enbas Saut and better suited for families with small children. The path involves only moderate climbs as it meanders through the rain forest with views of Piton St. Esprit, Mount Gimie and the Cannelles River. Since you stay at higher elevations most of the time, your chances of hearing or even seeing the St. Lucia parrot here are good. In the parking area, several tree species are labeled, some of which are indigenous to the island while others, like Caribbean pine and blue mahoe, were introduced to help prevent soil erosion.

Instead of retracing your steps back to the parking lot, you can follow this trail all the way over to the Quarter of Micoud on the west side of the island. For this trek of several hours, a guide is recommended to avoid getting lost on one of the numerous side trails. Try to arrange to have a vehicle waiting for you at the other end. Otherwise, you have to hitchhike or depend on a chain of mini-buses to get back to your hotel. Arrangements for a guide are made through the **Department of Forestry** *($25 with a guide;* ☎*450-2231).*

Petit Piton

Though it is not officially sanctioned, it is possible to climb Petit Piton, at your own risk, by way of a trail off Jalousie Road. It's a good idea to hire a guide who knows the way through the tricky sections. A number of experienced local men will offer to take you up, but make sure you settle on a price beforehand. At the base of the Piton a gentleman advertises guiding services. The climb is steep, very demanding and should only be attempted if you are physically fit and sure footed.

Gros Piton Nature Trail

The climb starts by going around the base of the Piton and gradually reaching the site of a former brigand camp on a small plateau. Soon after this point, the grade steepens sharply with a direct ascent up to the summit. Along the way, there are remains of brigand rock shelters, signal stations and look-outs. As you progress higher up the Piton, the trail passes through three distinct climatic environments. At the bottom, there is arid deciduous forest, which turns into a wide middle band of tropical rain forest, which in turn becomes elfin woodland and dwarf forest at the top. The spectacular view from the summit encompasses Vieux Fort, Choiseul and the mountains surrounding the peak of Mount Gimie to the northeast.

The hike to the top is certainly a challenge, but worth the effort. Like your mother said, however, you don't have to go all the way. The trail is divided into two sections: the first covers moderate terrain and keeps close to the Piton's base, while the other section involves a very demanding and sustained climb which is unsuitable

for the unfit or young children. For more details on treks up the Gros Piton you can call the local guides association *($13 or $52 with a guide; ☎459-3833)*.

Horseback Riding

Morne Coubaril Estate
☎459-7340

Trailrides are available on the beautiful grounds of Morne Coubaril Estate. Trips lasting from several hours to an entire week can be arranged. English- or Western-style riding lessons are also offered.

Sailing

Marigot Bay and Soufrière are both official ports of entry. There are five mooring areas in the Soufrière Marine Management Area (SMMA; see p 174 for explanation) between Anse Chastanet and Anse Mamin, Rachette Point, Soufrière Jetty, Malgretoute Beach (at the base of the Petit Piton) and the Beausejour area between the two Pitons. To moor your boat at one of these spots you must purchase a coral conservation permit from a SMMA officer.

The Moorings Yacht Charters
Marigot Bay
☎*451-4357 or 451-4014*
charters and full service marina facilities are available

Scuba Diving and Snorkelling

The southwest offers an incredible selection of diving sites for experts and beginners. The reefs and shipwrecks within the **Soufrière Marine Management Area (SMMA)** provide habitat for fish, coral and sponges. Snorkellers can enjoy reefs close to shore at Anse Chastanet, Soufrière Bay and Jalousie Resort.

Established in 1994, SMMA runs from Anse Jambon in the north to Anse L'Ivrogne in the south. It represents the laudable efforts of fishers, scuba-diving operators, hoteliers, yacht operators, government and community groups to use the rich marine resources of this area sustainably and equitably. It's similar to an ecological reserve but with a much broader mandate that focuses on the interdependence of environmental and

commercial sustainability. The coastline is divided into zones, each with its own assigned priority of use such as marine reserve, fishing or recreation. To protect marine flora and fauna, access to yacht moorings and dive sites is also controlled by SMMA through a permit system.

For information and permits contact:

SMMA
Marine VHF Radio Channel 16
P.O. Box 305, Bay St., Soufrière
☎*459-5500*
⇄*459-7799*
www.smma.org.lc

The following dive operators provide instruction, equipment rentals and boat charters:

*Humpbac
whale*

Soufrière

Scuba St. Lucia
Anse Chastanet Resort
☎*459-7755*

Frogs Eco-Dive Centre
Jalousie Hilton

☎459-7666 ext. 4024

Marigot Bay

Rosemond Trench Divers
☎451-4761

Whale-Watching

SMMA
☎459-5500
Whale-watching trips can be arranged through the SMMA.

Accommodations

Soufrière to Fond St. Jacques

Soufrière

 Cascara Guesthouse
$80
⊗, *sb*
South end of Church St. where the West Coast Rd. begins
☎459-7581
Located on a hill with splendid views of Soufrière Bay, Cascara Guesthouse offers budget travellers clean, comfortable and affordable rooms. In a quiet and private environment within walking distance of

town, guests can sip drinks on one of two balconies and save money by using the shared full kitchen. Not recommended for families with small children, only because the speeding traffic on Church Street could be hazardous.

Claudina's Guesthouse
$80
⊗, ℝ, *sb*
28 Bay St., Soufrière, between Clarke and High sts.
☎459-7567
Simple and clean, Claudina's Guesthouse is for budget travellers. It's located downtown and there is patio space in the backyard. Patrons also have the use of a common kitchen.

 Home Guesthouse
$80
⊗, ℝ, *sb*
Princess St., Soufrière, corner of Bridge and Princess sts., by the town square
☎459-7318
With a balcony overlooking the town square downtown and a sundeck on the roof, Home Guesthouse is great for people watching. Seven tidy and functional rooms are available at very reasonable rates. Guests have use of a common kitchen and spacious lounge area. Staff is personable and professional.

Sunset Guesthouse
$80
⊗, ℝ, K
20m (66ft) east of Bridge St. opposite
the fire station
☎459-7100
A short walk away from
downtown Soufrière, Sunset
Guesthouse provides clean,
basic accommodation close
to the beach. Guests have a
balcony overlooking the
street and a full kitchen.

La Mirage
$100
⊗, ℜ, ℝ
14 Church St., Soufrière, between
Sir Darnley Alexander and West
Quinlan sts.
☎/≈459-7010
Family-owned and oper-
ated, La Mirage provides
warm and attentive service
in a casual atmosphere.
Each of the rooms is mod-
ern and well kept with a
balcony to enjoy the sun
or take in the breeze. Furthermore, it's located in a
quiet area, even though
downtown Soufrière and
the waterfront are less than
a minute away.

Chez Camille
$169
⊗, ℝ, K
15 Church St., Soufrière, between Sir
Darnley Alexander and West Quilan
sts.
☎459-5379
≈459-5684
Chez Camille is a small,
modern, single floor home
in a quiet section of down

town Soufrière. It is basic
but clean and comfortable,
with a fully equipped
kitchen, small backyard and
verandah. The house has
no view of the water, but it
does offer complete inde-
pendence. Patrons are entitled to a 10% discount at
Camilla's restaurant.

Still Plantation Resort
$180
⊗, ≈, ℜ, ℝ, K
P.O. Box 246, Soufrière, Fond St.
Jacques Rd., second street after the
Soufrière River Bridge
☎459-7261
≈459-7301
On the original DuBoulay
estate, the Still Plantation
Resort is a beautiful 160ha
(400 acre) property close to
Fond St. Jacques. After 250
years, the DuBoulay family
still owns and operates the
estate, which gives the land
and the old stone buildings,
like the sugar mill and water wheel, a unique historical connection. Guests have
the picturesque grounds of
a working plantation to
explore and the option of
using the beach facilities at
The Still Beach Resort (see
p 177). The combination of
abundant natural space and
spacious rooms equipped
with full kitchens make this
a good choice for families
and large groups.

Hummingbird Beach Resort
$182

⊗, ≈, ℜ, ℝ, *Sb*

P.O. Box 280, Soufrière, Anse Chastanet Rd., north end of Bridge St.

☎*459-7232*

⇌*459-7033*

One of two beachfront hotels in Soufrière, Hummingbird Beach Resort offers guests a wonderful view of Petit Piton in a casual, but very comfortable atmosphere. Guests can choose from 11 cottage-style rooms, each with its own verandah by the pool. Expect nothing but friendly and attentive service.

La Haut Plantation
$208

⊗, ℜ, ℝ

P.O. Box 304, top of West Coast Rd. at the north ridge at Columbette

☎*459-7008*

⇌*459-5975*

Perched high above Soufrière, La Haut Plantation's breathtaking view takes in the entire valley, including the Sulphur Springs and both Pitons. On the grounds of a working plantation amid citrus trees, spices and coconut palms, the mountain air is fresh and invigorating. In a refurbished colonial home, six comfortable rooms are available, each with its own balcony and panoramic view. The intimacy afforded by this small hotel ensures guests receive friendly and attentive service.

The Still Beach Resort
$221

⊗, ℜ, ℝ

P.O. Box 246, Soufrière, Anse Chastanet Rd., north end of Bridge St.

☎*459-7261*

⇌*459-7301*

www.thestillresort.com

Owned by the DuBoulay family, The Still Beach Resort faces beautiful Soufrière Bay, and Petit Piton, and is just a few minutes walk away from Soufrière. The rooms are clean, functional and reasonably priced. Besides the beach, guests have easy access to a nearby dive site that is great for snorkelling. For a change of scenery, you can combine your visit with a stay at the DuBoulay's sister hotel, The Still Plantation Resort outside Soufrière (see p 176).

🛥 Mago Estate
$390 bkfst incl.

⊗, ≈, ℜ

P.O. Box 247, Soufrière, West Coast Rd., 200m (650ft) up the hill north of Bridge St.

☎*459-5880*

⇌*459-7352*

www.mago-hotel.com

Exceptional architectural design successfully integrates Mago Estate Hotel with its natural surroundings to create an inspiring and cozy atmosphere. The common room and restaurant are sheltered under a rock in the cliff face and the abundance of plants and flowers gives the sensation of being in a treehouse hideaway. There is a fresh-water pool with a splendid view of the harbour and Pitons, or guests can take the free shuttle down to the beach.

Anse Chastanet
$1,079 ½b
⊗, ℜ, ℝ, ☺, ◉
P.O. Box 7000, Soufrière, Anse Chastanet Rd., follow Bridge St. north around the bay to the end
☎*459-7000 or 459-7554*
⇥*459-7700*
www.ansechastanet.com

One of the most celebrated dive resorts in the Caribbean, Anse Chastanet is in a class by itself. All the rooms are open, well-designed, comfortable and built using local woods like mahogany, teak and wild breadfruit. Surrounded by tropical forest and a long strip of fine-sand beach, visitors can simply relax or take advantage of the exceptional diving facilities that include instruction, equipment rental and boat charters.

Marigot Bay

Canaries

The **St. Lucia National Trust** (☎*452-5005)* is currently building a number of interior campsites at Anse La Liberté, south of Canaries. Contact them for information.

Marigot Bay

Marigot Beach Club
$325
⊗, ≈, ℜ, K
P.O. Box 101, Castries, northwest side of the bay
☎*451-4974*
⇥*451-4973*

Next to the calm waters of picturesque Marigot Bay, the Marigot Beach Club feels like a remote tropical island. The rooms are open and pleasant with verandahs overlooking the coconut palms and sailboats in the lagoon. The hotel specializes in watersports, offering full-service diving facilities and free access to windsurfing boards, kayaks and snorkelling gear.

Auberge Marigot
$377 bkfst incl.
⊗, ≈, ℝ
P.O. Box 387, Castries, by the ferry parking lot; turn left up the south side of the bay
☎*451-4260*
⇥*451-4264*

Secluded on a rocky bluff overlooking Marigot Bay, Auberge Marigot offers relaxation and minimal distraction. The rooms are bright, spacious and breezy. Three hundred steps on a recently constructed path up the cliff connects you to the water below, where good snorkelling is available.

Oasis Marigot
$400

⊗, ≈, K

P.O. Box 387, Castries, north side of the bay above Marigot Beach Club

☎*451-4719*

⇆*451-4178*

Decorated with local art, tiles and wooden doors, the cottage-style rooms at Oasis Marigot are cozy and ideally situated with views of the ocean and harbour. The beach is only a short walk away or if you prefer, you can take the small trolley.

Seahorse Inn
$2,059/week bkfst incl.

⊗, ≈, ℜ

P.O. Box 1825, Castries, northeast end of the bay

☎*451-4436*

⇆*451-4872*

www.seahorse-inn.com

In a secluded part of the bay, the Seahorse Inn provides visitors with professional but personal guesthouse-style accommodation for a minimum stay of seven nights. The weekly rate includes airport transfer and ferry rides across Marigot Bay. The property is full of greenery where colourful birds flutter about the bright flowers and plants. The eight rooms are tastefully decorated, but you can also relax in the generous common room or out on the balcony.

Gros Piton

South of Soufrière

🏨 **Fond Doux Estate**
$182 bkfst incl.

⊗, ℜ

West side of West Coast Rd., shortly after Ladera Resort

☎*459-7545*

⇆*(809) 459-7882*

Situated on the site where the Battle of Rabot was fought more than 200 years ago, the Fond Doux Estate is not for those seeking a typical Caribbean vacation. It is however, ideal for people who enjoy nature, history, local culture and peaceful surroundings. Sleeping in one of two charmingly appointed rooms, with their old colonial-style verandahs, gabled roofs and wood shutters, is a history lesson in itself. The estate is still a working plantation so guests are encouraged to watch how some of its crops, like cocoa, are traditionally processed and to explore the lovely forests and hiking trails throughout the property.

Banana blossom

Soufrière and the West Coast

Stonefield Estates
$598
⊗, ≈, ℜ, *K*, ◙

P.O. Box 228, Soufrière, West Coast Rd., south of Soufrière past the viewing platform

☎*459-7037*

⇌*459-5550*

www.stonefieldvillas.com

An incredible view of Petit Piton dominates the scenery at Stonefield Estates, where guests enjoy stylish accommodation in beautiful surroundings. Each villa is well-furnished and fully equipped with modern kitchen appliances. Wooden shutters keep the cottages breezy and connected to all the natural beauty outside. Couples appreciate the privacy and romantic setting, but its also great for families and large groups. There is a free shuttle to Jalousie Beach.

Ladera Resort
$897 bkfst incl.
⊗, ≈, ℜ, ℝ, ◙

P.O. Box 225, Soufrière, West Coast Rd. south of the Sulphur Springs

☎*459-7323*

⇌*459-5156*

Classy and secluded, the villas of Ladera Resort stretch out along the edge of a high bluff between the Pitons. One of the most attractive aspects of this hotel's design is how well it is integrated with the surroundings. The use of local woods in construction, handicrafts created by Lucian artisans and rooms that open to a view of the Pitons creates an uplifting atmosphere. Most rooms come with their own small pool and shuttles to the beach run regularly. Since the premises are not considered playsafe, management prefers guests not to bring small children; those who do must sign a waiver.

Jalousie Hilton
$1,020
≡, ⊗, ≈, ⊛, ℜ, ℝ, ⊘, ◙

P.O. Box 251, Soufrière, off West Coast Rd. at the end of Jalousie Rd.

☎*459-7666*

⇌*459-7667*

www.jalousie-hilton.com

Nestled between the two Pitons, Jalousie Hilton is upscale, elegant and luxurious. Everything from a three-hole golf course and horseback riding to scuba diving and squash courts are available to guests. One hundred and fourteen very comfortable private villas are spaced out over 130ha (325 acres) on the grounds of a former sugar plantation. It's large and expensive, but it's the Hilton, where you expect to be pampered with the highest levels of service and nothing but the best facilities.

Restaurants

Soufrière to Fond St. Jacques

Soufrière

Purity Bakery
$
Mon-Sat 6am to 8pm
39 Church St., beside the Catholic church
☎*459-7325*
Purity Bakery serves freshly baked Creole baguettes and sweetcakes, cold drinks and instant coffee. It's a charming place to come in the morning for a baguette and cheese or later in the day for a snack. Don't forget to say "good morning."

Jah Lamb
$
Tue-Sat 12:30pm to 4:30pm
southeast corner of High and Bay sts.
Lunch at Jah Lamb's is your opportunity to sample some tasty Ital cuisine. In a Rastafarian style, a small selection of healthy vegetarian dishes is prepared daily using fresh ingredients. Besides Creole soups, dal with lentils or yellow peas, fruit juices and salad, there is delicious pizza topped with pumpkin, tomatoes, christophene, sweet peppers and cheese. The seat-

ing is limited, but take-out is available.

Chez Camille Fast Food
$
Mon-Sat noon to midnight
7 Bridge St., below Camilla's
☎*459-5379*
Chez Camille Fast Food offers simple and hearty Creole food, like roti or spiced chicken, in a laid-back environment. The crowd consists mainly of locals enjoying conversation and a cold beer. You can eat in or take-out, and ice cream cones are sold at the counter.

Fedo's
$
Mon-Sat noon to 9pm
Church St., between Sir Darnley Alexander and West Quilan sts.
☎*459-5220*
A popular lunch spot in Soufrière, Fedo's serves basic and affordable Creole fast food. Eat in or take-out.

Camilla's
$$$
7 Bridge St., between Sir Darnley Alexander and West Quilan sts.
☎*459-5379*
Located in the centre of Soufrière, Camilla's serves mainly Creole-style food at reasonable prices. The staff is warm and friendly, but the service slows on busy nights. Tables are also available on a balcony overlooking the street. This offers an affordable alternative when you crave a meal outside of

your hotel. Open until midnight.

La Mirage
$$$
Mon-Sat noon to 9pm
14 Church St., between Sir Darnley
Alexander and West Quilan sts.
☎459-7010
Family-owned and operated, La Mirage brings friendly, professional service to your table. The owners' 30 years of restaurant experience in England has created a reasonably priced selection of Creole and continental dishes.

Old Courthouse
$$$$
Baron Dr. opposite the jetty
☎459-5002
Set in a lovely century-old colonial building, the Old Courthouse offers fine dining, an art gallery and a gift shop. Patrons choose from a sophisticated menu of French, Creole and Southeast Asian dishes, such as Thai-style curry king prawns, spicy beef pepperpot stew or chicken tika with cucumber, mint and yogurt raita. Tourists from hotels or ships anchored in the harbour come here to enjoy a well-prepared meal on the terrace by Soufrière Bay. Upstairs, the old wood floors and stairs of the courthouse have been refinished and now underlie an art gallery featuring the works of local artisans.

The Lifeline
$$$
Anse Chastanet Rd. at the north end of
Bridge St.
☎459-7232
Located in the Hummingbird Beach Resort (see p 177), The Lifeline's outdoor terrace overlooks Soufrière Bay and has a wonderful view of Petit Piton. The open dining area lets in a pleasant seabreeze which harmonizes with the wood and stone decor, featuring the work of local woodcarvers and batik makers. A friendly and attentive staff serves a menu of Creole and French cuisine, including plates of freshly caught fish and a number of vegetarian selections.

The Still Plantation
$$$$
every day 8am to 5pm
Fond St. Jacques Rd. at The Still
Plantation Resort
☎459-7224
All the ingredients used by chefs at The Still Plantation—from the meat and fish to the fruits, spices and vegetables—are grown right on the premises. The dining area is open and comfortable. Patrons receive attentive service and quality ingredients in the selection of Creole, continental and North American-style dishes. Situated on one of the oldest estates in St. Lucia (see p 176), the Still Plantation, with its his-

toric buildings and beautiful surroundings is a great place for an after-dinner stroll.

The Still Beach Resort
$$$
Anse Chastanet Rd. at the north end of Bridge St.
☎459-7261
At The Still Beach Resort, diners eat comfortably and casually on a patio near the beach. The menu features a good selection of Creole dishes, including a spicy local recipe for pepper pot stew and conch lambi. Chefs prepare your meal using fresh fruits and vegetables from The Still Plantation in Soufrière.

La Haut Plantation
$$$$
2.5km (1.5mi) north of Soufrière, top of West Coast Rd.
☎459-7008
Perched on a high ridge above Soufrière, La Haut is renowned as much for its food as it is for its dramatic view. Diners enjoy meals and professional service on one of three balconies overlooking the Soufrière Valley and the Pitons. The menu contains a broad selection of well prepared continental and Creole cuisine made with herbs and produce grown on the property. It's a worthwhile dining excursion, especially in the evening.

Mago Estate
$$$$
dinner only
West Coast Rd., 200m (650ft) north of Soufrière
☎453-5880
In a romantic natural setting, Mago Estate serves a set menu nightly. Several options are available, like fresh fish in ginger and garlic sauce or Creole chicken. Although it is worth a visit for the food and service, its incredible architecture is what really sets this restaurant apart from the rest. Built into a rock face with a stunning view of the bay and Pitons, the dining area is surrounded by tropical plants and flowers with a treetop nook to enjoy a drink before the meal. Reservations are required.

Anse Chastanet
$$$$
end of Anse Chastanet Rd., north side of the bay
☎459-7000
Set on the beach under a sheltered patio, Anse Chastanet's Trou au Diable Restaurant is surrounded by the sounds of the forest and the surf lapping up to shore. The outdoor concept is relaxing and showcases the resort's beautiful location. Patrons choose from a large menu, consisting of American, European and Creole dishes, that satisfies even the fussiest of tastes. A truly inspiring dining experience.

Marigot Bay

Château Mygo
$$

Marigot Bay Rd. by the ferry
☎451-4772

In a small cozy cottage, Château Mygo serves "St. Lucian style home cooking" in a friendly unassuming atmosphere. All of the meals are prepared using local ingredients and served on a lovely terrace surrounded by flowers and tropical plants. The mainly Creole menu features some spicy local stew recipes and an interesting selection of fusion items like Caribbean burritos.

JJ's Paradise
$$$

first right off Marigot Beach Rd.
☎451-4076

Fun and casual, JJ's Paradise is a popular spot for Lucians and tourists alike, who come to relax and enjoy hearty Creole and mainly North American-style food. Wednesday nights everyone converges here to enjoy grilled seafood. There is a lovely boardwalk linking the restaurant to the harbour, where boats can be moored. Patrons receive a complimentary one-way taxi ride.

The Shack
$$$

south side of Marigot Bay, park by the ferry
☎451-4145

On a jetty in the middle of beautiful Marigot Bay, The Shack is a wonderful seaside dining spot. The simple but stylish decor makes use of wood and warm lighting to create an intimate ambiance. The menu covers a wide selection of items from shrimp calypso, St. Lucia accra and callaloo soup to roast beef sandwiches, nachos or spinach fettucini. You can moor your boat to the restaurant's dock.

Doolittle's Restaurant
$$$

north shore of Marigot Bay, take the ferry across
☎451-4974

Doolittle's combines a good selection of seafood dishes like prawns in local Marie Rose dressing. Tables are set on an open terrace by the water with a view of the sea and harbour. Accessible by water.

Gros Piton

South of Soufrière

Dasheene
$$$$

West Coast Rd. at Ladera Resort
☎459-7323

Set on a ridge overlooking the valley between the

Pitons, Dasheene offers a stunning view of St. Lucia's most famous landmarks. The lovely terrace was built using locally produced wood and tile, as were the furnishings and art decorations. Local ingredients are also used to create an interesting selection of Creole dishes, like coconut and christophene soup or internationally inspired fare such as pasta antoinette, tagliatelle pasta with a cream sauce of mushrooms, basil and garden vegetables, topped with sundried tomatoes. In the evening, warm candlelight enhances the mood of a romantic dining experience. Dasheene is also open early for breakfast.

The Plantation Room
$$$$
dinner only
Jalousie Hilton Resort, Plantation Rd.
off West Coast Rd.
☎**459-7666**
Classy and refined, The Plantation Room serves foods of the Mediterranean and Far East. In a romantic and intimate atmosphere, it offers fine dining with above-standard service. Of course, you are required to dress appropriately for the occasion: a collared shirt with long pants for the gentlemen and cocktail dresses or skirts for the ladies.

Entertainment

Soufrière to Fond St. Jacques

Soufrière

Quiet throughout the week, Soufrière lets loose on Friday and Saturday nights when the whole town gets into a festive mood. Crowds gather around the loud speakers at the corner of Clarke and Bay streets. Every so often, there is also something happening at the town hall on Bridge Street, with live music, DJs or a community event. You'll know something is going on by the vendors and people crowded outside along the street. They always appreciate another paying customer, so feel free to enter. It's a great opportunity to experience local culture and support the community at the same time. Normally, the admission price is about $10 to $20 which explains why most of the youth hang around outside.

Otherwise, nightlife is limited to regular live shows at the hotels. Wednesday and Friday nights live island

Soufrière and the West Coast

music is featured at Anse Chastanet (*Anse Chastanet Rd., follow Bridge St. north around the bay to the end;* ☎459-7354) and Thursday nights the same is available at the Pier Restaurant at the Jalousie Hilton (*off West Coast Rd. at the end of Jalousie Rd.;* ☎459-7666).

Marigot Bay

JJ's Paradise
every day 9am to midnight
first right on Marigot Bay Rd.
☎**451-4076**
An easygoing, friendly atmosphere makes it a pleasure to relax and enjoy a drink at JJ's Paradise. On Wednesday and Friday nights, the live music is popular with both locals and tourists. The patio pool, a small zoo in the backyard and some tasty local spiced-rum brews at the bar are all part of the fun.

Shopping

Saturday is market day in Soufrière. Vendors line up their fresh fruits and vegetables along Bay Street in the early morning. It's definitely worth a visit for both the food and people-watching opportunities.

Livity Art Studio
every day 8am to 7pm
West Coast Rd. north of Soufrière in Columbette
☎**459-3007**
In a traditional Carib-style building, Livity Art Studio offers, among other things, coal pots, old fashioned white cedar chairs, grass mats and a collection of finely crafted wooden masks and sculptures carved from the local red cedar and mabwe trees.

The Old Courthouse
every day 10am to 11pm
Bay St. next to the jetty
☎**459-5002**
Located in Soufrière, The Old Courthouse has a colourful collection of batik designs on the upper floor along with some local crafts and various T-shirts made with Lucian cotton.

White hibiscus

Vieux Fort and the South

Travelling south from Soufrière toward Vieux Fort and the South ★★ is like leaving one world and entering another.

While the mountains and dense forests recede into the interior, sections of the highway flatten into long straight lines, like runways. The land spreads out into open fields, wrinkled in places with narrow ravines leading to the Caribbean Sea. This is a much drier landscape; the air thins and the tropical humidity disappears along with the deep saturated greens of the southwest.

Arawaks and Caribs established numerous settlements in the south for good reason. There's plenty of fish in the ocean, crabs and crayfish in the mangrove swamps, and an abundance of grass, timber and clay for building materials. Later, the early French settlers turned the south

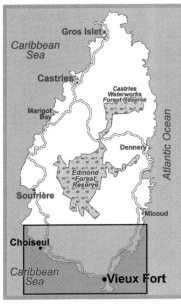

into a booming agricultural region for cotton and tobacco, and when St. Lucia's sugar bonanza started, it began on estates in the south such as La Perle, Sapphire and Balenbouche. Now, Vieux Fort's agricultural importance has been eclipsed by its growth as an industrial and shipping centre.

Fewer tourists take the time to explore the far south. Tourism is less developed, but it also lacks the intrusiveness which is so much a part of the experience in the northern areas. There are excellent beaches here, like Anse de Sables, famous for its windsurfing, but no crowds. Hotels in the smaller southern towns of Laborie and Piaye offer more than just quiet relaxation. They offer a genuine feeling of seclusion from the everyday world and an opportunity to connect with Lucian people and learn about local culture.

The southern region is unique on the island for its coastal reserves, where nature lovers have the chance to experience the natural environment of St. Lucia beyond its forests. On the Maria Islands, you will find the extremely rare *zandoli te* lizard and the *couresse* snake. A drive around Man Kote will introduce you to a mangrove swamp. There is also the adventure of exploring the ravines of the Dorée and Piaye rivers and then the exhilarating vista from Moule à Chique.

Finding Your Way Around

The West Coast Highway is the only north-south road along the Caribbean coast. In Vieux Fort, after looping around the southern edge of Hewanorra International Airport, it becomes the East Coast Highway, which is also the only north-south route on the Atlantic side of the island. The main thoroughfare in Vieux Fort is Clarke Street, which runs through the centre of town from the West Coast Highway down to the waterfront. The two tours in this chapter begin in Vieux Fort. Tour A takes you on the West Coast Highway north to Choiseul. Tour B starts on top of Moule à Chique Peninsula and then heads north on New Dock Road, out of Vieux Fort on the East Coast Highway to Savannes Bay Nature Reserve.

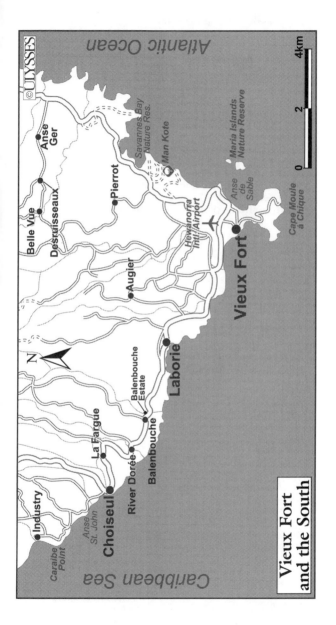

Vieux Fort
and the South

By Car

Driving in the south is less intense, without the steep climbs and sharp turns you find in the central mountainous regions. Between Choiseul and Vieux Fort the road is rough in sections, but the East Coast Highway is in very good shape and is the quickest route to Castries. The secondary roads that follow the bigger rivers inland from the main highway are worth exploring. In this region, they tend to connect with one another so it's possible to travel great distances across the interior.

Car Rental Agencies

Hewanorra International Airport

Avis
☎454-6325
⇌453-1536

Budget
☎454-5311
⇌454-7579

Cool Breeze Jeep-Car Rental
☎454-7898
⇌459-5309

Hertz
☎454-9636
⇌452-8980

St. Lucia National Car Rental Services
☎454-6699

Vieux Fort

Ojay Car Rentals
☎454-6665
⇌454-9665

By Plane

Most of St. Lucia's international flights are received at **Hewanorra International Airport** (☎454-6355/454-6782) on the outskirts of Vieux Fort. You enter the airport from the East Coast Highway, north of the runway. Plenty of taxis are available during arrival times so there should be no problems getting to your hotel wherever it may be on the island. A more affordable option is the minibus, which you get to by walking to the main road. Minibuses on the west side of the road go directly to Castries. For Soufrière, take a minibus on the east side into Vieux Fort and then transfer to the Soufrière bus which is around the corner by the Shell gas station (ask the first driver to show you where to wait).

Helicopter operators based at George FL Charles Airport in Vigie offer tours and a shuttle service between both airports.

Paradise Helicopters
☎450-9203

St. Lucia Helicopters
☎458-1390

By Bus

Minibuses operate regularly
out of Vieux Fort along
both coastal highways. For
Soufrière and Castries,
minibuses wait to fill up
along the main highway at
the east end of town. For
local routes, busses wait by
Independence Square on
Clarke Street.

Major Bus Routes

No.2 *($6)*
Vieux Fort-Castries

No.4 *($8)*
Vieux Fort-Soufrière

By Taxi

Taxis can be hired to shuttle you to the airport or for
tours around the island. All
rates are fixed according to
government standards.

**Hewanorra Airport
Southern Taxi Association**
☎*454-6136*

**Vieux Fort
New Frontier Taxi Association**
☎*454-5555*

Taxi Boutique
☎*454-7084*

Practical Information

Tourist Information

St. Lucia Tourist Board
*Every day from noon until the
last flight of the day*
Hewanorra Airport
☎*454-6644*

Money and Banking

Hewanorra
International Airport

National Commercial Bank
Every day noon to last flight
☎*454-7780*

Vieux Fort

Bank of Nova Scotia
ATM available
New Dock Rd., by JQ Charles Mall
☎*454-6314*

Barclays
ATM available
New Dock Rd., by JQ Charles Mall
☎*454-6255*

**Canadian Imperial Bank of
Commerce**
ATM available
East Coast Hwy., by the roundabout at
New Dock Rd.
☎*456-2422*

Vieux Fort
and the South

Royal Bank of Canada
ATM available
New Dock Rd., by JQ Charles Mall
☎ *454-5804*

St. Lucia Cooperative Bank
Commercial St., two blocks west of the
police station
☎ *454-6213*

Black Bay

Caribbean Banking Corporation
Gablewoods Mall South
☎ *454-7264*

Mail

There are two major post
offices in this region:

Black Bay
Gablewoods Mall South
Mon-Fri 9am to 5:30pm

Vieux Fort
north end of Theodore St.
Mon-Fri 8:30am to 4:30pm

Telecommunications

In Vieux Fort, the most
reliable public telephones
are located outside the post
office on Theodore Street.

Pharmacies

R.J. Clarke
☎ *454-7556*

Julian's
☎ *454-9598*

Minvielle and Chastanet
☎ *458-8154*

Police

Vieux Fort
corner of Commercial St. and
Thomas Ave.
☎ *454-6333*

Photography

There are no photography
stores in this region, but
you can purchase film and
batteries at pharmacies or
dry goods shops in Vieux
Fort and at Gablewoods
Mall in Black Bay.

Supermarkets

Julian's
Gablewoods Mall South

JQ's
Commercial St.

JQ Charles Shopping Mall
New Dock Rd.

Exploring

There are two tours in this
chapter: **Tour A: Vieux Fort to
Choiseul ★★** brings you
north from Vieux Fort to
Choiseul along the island's
Caribbean coast. **Tour B:
Moule à Chique to Savannes**

Bay ★★ is shorter and explores the nature reserves and attractions surrounding Vieux Fort.

Tour A:
Vieux Fort to Choiseul

Hurricane Allen inflicted severe damage on the town of **Vieux Fort** ★ in 1980. As a result, much of this sprawling community was built quite recently, but in the older section of town, nearest the water, there are still many charming colonial buildings, such as the police station on Commercial Street. Although there are many attractions on the outskirts of Vieux Fort, the town itself has little to offer tourists. Due to Hewanorra International Airport and the large port facilities located here, Vieux Fort is mainly a shipping and industrial centre.

The tour begins along the waterfront at the end of Clarke Street. Straight ahead is the new fisheries complex, built with financial assistance from Japan. Follow the dirt road north by the water, past the fish market to a makeshift community for fishers, who stay here to get an early start in the morning. If you stop and take a walk along the beach you might see some of them cleaning the day's catch for dinner, mending nets, or making one of their finely crafted fishtraps.

When you reach the West Coast Highway, turn left to go north alongside the airport runway. During the Second World War, the United States leased 400ha (1000 acres) from the Lucian government to build a military base in Vieux Fort. Shortly after, Beanfield Airstrip was built, along with a hospital and shipping dock. This installation served as a refueling station for flights to North Africa and a place for wounded soldiers returning from action could convalesce. The United States closed its base on the island in 1960, and in 1971, the airstrip was reopened with the help of Canadian aid as **Hewanorra International Airport**. Now instead of sounding like a small town in Idaho, it has a Carib name meaning Land of the Iguana.

After you cross Vieux Fort River, the highway cuts inland across a barren plain dotted with grazing horses and cattle. At Black Bay, the land rises gradually into dry scrubland and the road starts winding in and out of a series of ravines. A left turn at the first major junction brings you into the centre of Laborie.

Vieux Fort
and the South

Cocoa Tea

Cocoa tea is a popular hot drink in St. Lucia and across the Caribbean. You can find all the necessary spices and bars of locally grown cocoa at markets around St. Lucia. Before buying, check to see that the spices are fresh and pungent.

Ingredients

premix 1/2 teaspoon flour in 1/4 cup water
6 tablespoons of grated fresh cocoa
2 cups milk
2 cups water
lime peel
cinnamon, nutmeg, cloves and brown sugar to taste

Mix water, nutmeg and lime peel in a pot and bring to a boil. Add grated cocoa and let simmer. Then, add milk and the flour mixture. Dissolve and simmer on low heat. Do not let the milk boil. Remove from heat and let the grounds fall. Makes 3 mugs.

The French founded a set tlement at **Laborie ★★** in the early 18th century, calling it Anse de Islet à Carret because of all the sea turtles that nested on the large sandbar in the bay (*carret* being French for a type of turtle). The town was later renamed in honour of Baron de Laborie, governor of St. Lucia from 1784-89.

In the old part of town, near the waterfront, many picturesque wooden homes and buildings line the street. The beach is full of fishing boats and multi-coloured nets are strung out in preparation for the next outing. The coral reef in the bay is what makes this area such a bountiful fishing ground, as well as a popular diving site.

One of the oldest buildings in town is the community centre, on Main Street. Buil in 1839 by the Mico Trust, i was one of the first schools in St. Lucia. By opening schools and teacher's colleges throughout the 19th century, this British charity was at the forefront of making primary education available to former slaves in the Caribbean. At that time, very few blacks had the resources to send their children to school and even fewer were literate themselves. The Trust's campaign was resisted by many planters across the Caribbean who feared education would ultimately draw their main source of labour away from the fields. In St. Lucia, the Catholic church eventually took over full control of the education system.

The tour continues north on Main Street up a small hill towards a church and cemetery, where it eventually merges with the West Coast Highway. The road follows a flat coastal plain that lies between the sea to the west and the hills to the east. During the early colonial period, the large estates in this area grew tobacco, cassava, cotton and ginger before turning their operations over to sugar cane and later to other crops

like coffee, cocoa and coconuts. Now with labour costs so high, the estates no longer find it profitable to grow crops on a large scale so much of the land is left unused. The Lucian government is also battling a mite infestation that has severely affected a number of coconut plantations in the region.

After a series of sharp curves through the Piaye River Ravine, you come upon **Balenbouche Estate ★ ★ ★** (☎455-1244) on the west side of the highway. A long tree-lined driveway, bright with purple flowers, leads to the plantation's main house, or the Great House, as they were known in the British Caribbean in the 18th century. Built by a French planter over 200 years ago, this wonderfully preserved home is still inhabited by the present owners of the estate.

Once a large cotton and sugar plantation, Balenbouche is now a family-run farm and guesthouse. If you call in advance, it's possible to arrange for lunch or dinner to be served and you

Traditional coal pot stove

can also take the opportunity to look around the property, with its tropical flowers, avocado trees, star and passion fruit, several colonial buildings, such as the old cotton house, and two secluded beaches. A short forest trail in the ravine reveals the plantation's original mill works and a giant water wheel standing over two stories high, imported from G.W. Fletcher in London. An elaborate aqueduct system channelled water from the Balenbouche River to the wheel, creating a power source for the sugar-cane squeezer.

Back at the highway, a left turn leads you down a long straightaway broken by a short descent to cross the River Dorée. Of the many narrow ravines formed by water draining out of the wetter interior regions, the **River Dorée ★★** is one of the more dramatic. It is over 45m (150ft) deep and only 6m (20ft) across in some sections. Along the river's edges the vegetation thickens, but as the road swerves sharply inland, the terrain quickly returns to isolated pockets of short trees and grassy fields.

Students from the surrounding area attend the **Choiseul Arts and Crafts Centre ★★** *(Mon-Fri 8:30am to 4:30pm, Sat 10am to 2pm; ☎459-3226)* in La Fargue to become artisans of traditional handi-crafts. Tourists can also arrange to participate in pottery, woodcarving and grass weaving workshops lasting from 1hr to an entire week.

On display in the store are coal pot stoves and cook-pots made using the Carib technique of first drying them in the sun and covering them with brush on an open fire. Some items, like the handbaskets, involve a lengthy process of collecting and preparing the materials. Both are constructed with the roots of the *awali* and *ti kanot*, two species of creeper vines found only in the rain forest. Each has to be boiled before it can be used, and the *ti kanot* roots are also soaked in water for two weeks and then pounded on rocks to remove their rough skin.

Further along, the highway descends a steep hill to the quaint fishing town of **Choiseul ★★**, on the other side of the Grande Rivière Choiseul. In the early days of Caribbean exploration, it was dubbed Anse Citron because of all the limes growing here, which sailors used to fight scurvy. French settlers celebrated the Treaty of Paris in 1763 by renaming this town after the duke of Choiseul, France's minister of foreign affairs at the negotiating table in Europe.

A quick left turn after the bridge leads into Choiseul and a quiet cove with a coconut palm beach that is usually covered with fishing boats. Wooden plank homes and shops with bright silver aluminum roofs line the road to the waterfront. The Catholic church was built in 1906.

The tour continues north through town and up the hill. On your left is a sign indicating the presence of a petroglyph figure, most likely of Arawak origin, carved into a rock. The clay soil in this area attracted a succession of indigenous groups who used it to make pottery and cooking utensils.

A short distance up the road, take the next left towards the coast through an area known as Portalese to **Anse John ★★** (see p 200). North of the beach, a dramatic wall of sandy cliffs leads to Caraibe Point where the last of St. Lucia's Carib population once lived. In 1774, only four families remained, since most had died of disease or left for reservations on Dominica and St. Vincent. There are no pure Caribs on the island today. They mixed with the African slave population, but some of their physical features live on in the faces of certain residents.

Return to Vieux Fort along the same route.

Tour B:
Moule à Chique
to Savannes Bay

This tour heads west on New Dock Road towards the port at Vieux Fort Bay. The shipping dock was built by the United States as a military base during the Second World War. It has since been refurbished after having been severely damaged by Hurricane Allen in 1980. Today, Vieux Fort is St. Lucia's most important shipping facility next to Castries.

Keep left at the fork to the jetty, and climb the steep winding road to the top of **Moule à Chique ★★★** Peninsula, where an abandoned telecommunications station offers one of the most exciting views on the island. Even if you decide to walk, it's definitely worth the effort.

From this exposed position 219m (730ft) above sea level, you can feel the force of the northeast tradewinds, which have bent the vegetation and smoothed the peninsula into a rounded

Vieux Fort and the South

green surface. Directly south of the station, perched on the edge of Cape Moule à Chique, is the world's second-highest lighthouse. Rising out of the northwest are the Pitons and mountainous country of the forest reserves. To the east, looking like two stranded ships, the Maria Islands break the white capped waves by Pointe Sable. A rim of honey-coloured sand marks the eastern shoreline stretching north to the wide mouth of Savannes Bay and Saltibus Point, where it breaks into a series of tiny coves. North of the airport, the Vieux Fort River cuts through the community of La Resource and then disappears into the interior of the island as

it widens into hills and ridges.

Having seen the route from above, return to New Dock Road and veer right at the roundabout towards the east coast. The road curves northward at **Anse de Sables ★★** (see p 200), where it's likely the first Europeans landed on St. Lucia in 1605. They were English sailors aboard the *Olive Branch* in search of food and water. They stayed only a short time before a Carib attack forced them to abandon their camp.

A short distance from shore is **Maria Islands Nature Reserve ★★★** (*$81 for a guide and boat ride; closed mid-May to end July; Mon-Fri 9am to 5pm; ☎454-5014*). In the interest of protecting the islands' delicate eco-systems, the St. Lucia National Trust strictly controls access to the reserve. A 2.5hr tour, accompanied by a registered guide, can be arranged through the Maria Islands Nature Centre, at the west end of Anse de Sables. You must, however, book at least 24hrs in advance. The reserve closes from mid-May to the end of July,

Red mangrove tree

when large numbers of sea and land birds nest on the islands.

This unique and enjoyable excursion involves an exciting boat ride and a short hike across a tiny windswept island in the Caribbean Sea. If you own snorkelling gear, bring it along to explore the reef near the beach on Maria major. Birdwatchers will find plenty of species to add to their lists. There are terns, doves, redbilled tropic birds and, of course, magnificent frigate birds. Amid the rocks, grass and cacti, researchers have identified more than 120 different plants on both islands. The real star, however, is the rare *zandoli te* lizard, with its bright-blue tail and the St. Lucia racer or *couresse* snake, which can only be found on these two islands. Biologists believe the *couresse* probably inhabited the mainland until Europeans introduced the mongoose to rid St. Lucia of its venomous snakes.

Our tour continues along the East Coast Highway, which bends around the runway at Pointe Sable. In the late 17th century, the Dutch constructed fortifications here to protect themselves from Carib attacks while they loaded their ships with fresh supplies of wood and water.

The road curves inland past a group of cottages used during the Second World War by U.S. military personnel stationed at Beanfield Air Base. After Hewanorra Airport, you can also see the other abandoned U.S.-built runway.

Some 200m (650ft) farther, turn right onto a rough dirt road into **Man Kote ★★**, one of the few large mangrove swamps left in St. Lucia. The National Trust plans to establish Pointe Sable National Park and integrate Man Kote into a chain of coastal parks from Savannes Bay to Moule à Chique. At present, the only access into this extremely fragile ecosystem is by a road skirting around the edge of the two swamp areas.

Mangrove trees are actually a type of tropical evergreen that thrives in the salt water, mud and sand of coastal rivers and basins. Among the many other trees and shrubs in the swamps, the red mangrove is the most distinctive, with its large, aerated root systems that anchor the tree in the soil beneath the shallow water. Ecologically, these swamps are an important habitat and breeding area for birds, insects, crustaceans and fish. If you follow the access road all the way into the mangrove, there is also

Vieux Fort
and the South

a rough beach area where you can swim.

When you leave Man Kote, turn right onto the East Coast Highway through the community of St. Urbain to **Savannes Bay Nature Reserve ★★**. Beside the Cool Breeze restaurant, you can arrange for a boat tour of the reserve for roughly $52 per person, with cheaper rates available for groups of six.

Scorpion Island sits in the middle of the bay, sheltered from rough seas by Burgot Point in the south and the long peninsula of Saltibus Point, which reaches out across the northeast. A mangrove covers much of the bay's north shore, while the wetland of Eau Piquant, on the south shore, is particularly good for bird-watching, attracting species such as the white breasted thrasher, and green herons as well as cattle and snowy egrets. A coral reef off of Saltibus Point is one of the reasons Savannes Bay is also known for good fishing.

To return to Vieux Fort, head back south on the East Coast Highway.

Beaches

Anse John

Anse John is a well-maintained beach with plenty of soft sand, but be careful during rainstorms, as there are manchineel trees along the path to the beach (see p 60).

Anse de Sables

A popular spot among locals and tourists, Anse de Sables has a long sandy beach and rolling waves that add a bit of excitement to a refreshing swim in the ocean. Many windsurfing enthusiasts are also drawn to this bay by the combination of strong winds and high waves. There are restaurants on the beach for drinks or a meal by the water.

Outdoor Activities

Cycling

Bicycles can be rented for $5 per hr at the **Reef Café** (☎454-7400) on Anse de Sables.

Scuba Diving

There are two diving sites in the south at Pointe Sable and Laborie Bay. Equipment and lessons can be arranged through **Club Med** (☎454-6546/47/48).

Windsurfing

Anse de Sables is also rightfully known as Windsurfers Beach. Its ideal conditions are beginning to attract international interest, so windsurfing enthusiasts will appreciate the opportunity to get out on their boards.

Reef Café / Club Mistral
Anse de Sables, middle of beach
☎*454-7400)*
Operating under the name Club Mistral, the Reef Café offers a windsurfing program. Instruction for all skill levels is available and boards can be rented for $38 per hr.

Club Med
Anse de Sables, middle of beach
☎*454-6546/47/48*
Club Med rents boards for $110 per day with lunch included. They have a facility on the beach, but you have to book this package at the hotel. A free shuttle leaves every 15min for the hotel from beside the Reef Café.

Accommodations

Vieux Fort to Choiseul

Vieux Fort

St. Martin's Guesthouse
$108
⊗
Clarke St. opposite minibus stands at Independence Square
☎*454-6674*
The only accommodation in the centre of Vieux Fort, St. Martin's Guesthouse has small but well-kept rooms. There is a common eating

area for guests and tables set up in a flower garden in the backyard. Be forewarned, however that the elderly woman who runs the place insists guests be in by 11pm. Meals available on request.

Il Pirata
$156
≡, ℜ
P.O. Box 296, West Coast Hwy., 1km (0.6mi) northwest of Vieux Fort
☎454-6610

Located on the site of what was once the watersports pavillion for Sandals Halcyon, Il Pirata has several basic but clean rooms available. The surroundings are quiet, with ample green space, and the beach is just steps from your door.

Kimatrai Hotel
$175
≡, ℜ, ℑ
P.O. Box 238, Vieux Fort, western end of New Dock Rd.
☎454-6328
⇌454-3038

Overlooking Vieux Fort Bay, the Kimatrai Hotel has wonderful views of the Caribbean Sea and Moule à Chique Peninsula. The standard rooms come with adequate furnishings and several small cottages should also be available in the foreseeable future. Only a short distance from downtown Vieux Fort, it provides a convenient base for exploring the region.

Laborie

Mirage Hotel
$169
⊗, K, ℜ
north end of the beach in Laborie Bay
☎/⇌455-9763

Surrounded by the sand and surf of Laborie Bay, guests at the Mirage can enjoy the tranquil ambiance of a small beach hotel away from the tourist scene found elsewhere on the island. Each of the rooms is spacious, comfortable, tastefully furnished and comes equipped with extra cots and a full kitchen, which makes them ideal for families or large groups. The beach is only a few steps away and the snorkelling in the bay is fantastic. You can enjoy meals on the terrace with its cozy driftwood-style furniture and tables shaded with palm leaves, or on the patio of your room.

Piaye

Margaret's Guesthouse
$60 bkfst incl.
⊗
Piaye, unsurfaced road off the West Coast Hwy.
☎455-1801

Margaret's offers the cheapest rooms in the area. It's basic but clean, comfortable and only a short distance to the beach. This makes a good base for exploring the Dorée River gorge or the Piaye River.

Loretta's Place
$150 bkfst incl.
⊗, ≈, ℜ
West Coast Hwy. south of the Piaye
River and Balenbouche Estate
☎*455-1710*
⇄*455-1017*
Situated midway between
Vieux Fort and Choiseul,
Loretta's offers travellers
bed and breakfast accom-
modation with personalized
but professional service.
The large, comfortable
rooms are laid out around a
swimming pool with a view
of the Caribbean Sea. There
is also a beach nearby.

Balenbouche Estate
$175
⊗, ℜ, K
P.O. Box 707, Vieux Fort, West Coast
Hwy. north of Piaye
☎*455-1244*
⇄*455-1342*
Amid the history and natural beauty of a 200-year-old
working plantation,
Balenbouche Estate (see
p 195), offers visitors a different kind of island experience. Rooms furnished with
period antiques are available in the well-preserved
18th-century estate house or
for more private and independent accommodation,
there are several unique
villas. Each was designed
by the owner with an em-
phasis on creating very
open and natural environ-
ments, with spacious lay-
outs, wooden shutters on
the doors and windows,
and even outdoor showers

built out of a small rock
garden. There is also much
to explore on this 60ha (150
acre) property, including a
nature trail, two beaches,
lovely gardens, historic
buildings and the ruins of
an old sugar mill.

Choiseul

Miss Lucy's
$100 ($75 without shower)
⊗, K
La Fargue, south of Choiseul on the
West Coast Hwy.
☎*459-3142*
Located 5min from Choi-
seul, Miss Lucy's apartment-
style rooms are good for
those planning to work or
stay for an extended period.
The disadvantage is the
noise from the traffic on the
highway, but for some, this
may be outweighed by the
complete independance this
establishment provides in a
part of the island that rarely
sees tourists. If you stay
here, consider taking one of
the workshops at the
Choiseul Arts and Crafts
Centre (see p 206).

Moule à Chique to Savannes Bay

Cloudnest Cottages
$70
⊗, ℜ, K
Beanfield, East Coast Hwy., 500m
(1,500ft) north of Pointe Sable
☎*484-1785*
Occupying former resi-
dences of the U.S. military

base, Cloudnest Cottages are a little run down, but still very functional. For a very reasonable price, you have several large rooms, a full-size kitchen and a verandah looking out onto the water. It's quiet and located within walking distance of Vieux Fort and the beach. This is an ideal place for a group of budget travellers.

Kabran Hotel
$156 bkfst incl.
≡

P.O. Box 239, Vieux Fort, East Coast Hwy., 100m (328ft) east of New Dock Rd.
☎*454-3331*
⇌*454-7673*

The Kabran Hotel offers clean, comfortable and modern rooms mainly to airline personnel and business travellers. There is nothing extraordinary about this hotel's atmosphere or location except that it happens to be a cheaper alternative to the pricier hotels close to the airport.

Skyway Inn
$208
≡, ≈, ℜ
P.O. Box 353, Vieux Fort, East Coast Hwy., opposite the airport
☎*454-7111*
⇌*454-7116*
www.st-lucia.de

Only minutes from Hewanorra Airport, the Skyway Hotel attracts a large clientele of airline personnel and business travellers. All of the rooms

are comfortable and come with a balcony. Its modern facilities, professional service and pool are other reasons why it is so popular.

Juliette's Lodge
$247
≡, ≈, ℜ
P.O. Box 482, Vieux Fort, East Coast Hwy., 500m (1,500ft) south of the airport
☎*454-5300*
⇌*454-5305*
www.cavip.com

Located 5min from Anse de Sables, Juliette's Lodge offers quiet surroundings with few distractions. All 16 modern rooms are clean, comfortably furnished and have a large balcony with views of the Atlantic Ocean and Moule à Chique.

Restaurants

Vieux Fort to Choiseul

Vieux Fort

Destiny Café
$
closed Sun
Clarke Ave., across from the minibus stands at Independence Square
Destiny Café serves basic home-style Creole food at very affordable prices. There are several vegetarian meals, including roti and

salads, and a selection of fresh fruit juices. You can either eat in at the few tables on hand or take out. Its clientele is mainly locals enjoying a quick meal and some good music.

Il Pirata
$$$$
closed Mon
West Coast Hwy., 1km (0.6mi) north of Clarke Ave.
☎*454-6610*

Run by a friendly Italian couple, Il Pirata offers nothing but tasty authentic Italian cuisine, like chicken breast milanese and mushrooms trifolati. Patrons dine by the sea in an open and breezy atmosphere, with shaded tables also available on a terrace closer to the beach. Add to this the professional service, and it's a great place to enjoy a romantic meal and watch the sunset.

Laborie

Bois Coco Restaurant and Bar
$$
Tue-Sun from 11am, Mon from 6pm
Testiny Hwy., northern junction of West Coast Hwy. and road into Laborie
☎*455-9122*

Situated by the roadside, Bois Coco is a small, unassuming restaurant that makes a good lunch stop on your tour of the coast. Inside the funky bamboo exterior, the atmosphere is casual and relaxed. Along-

side beer, cocktails and fruit juices is a menu of simple fare like roast chicken, the "catch of the day," burgers and fries.

Moule à Chique to Savannes Bay

Reef Café
$$$
closed Mon
Anse de Sables, opposite the runway
☎*454-3418*

Situated right on the beach, the Reef Café caters mainly to tourists from nearby hotels. There is a wonderful view of Anse de Sables and Moule à Chique from tables on the balcony. Naturally, with the beach only a few steps away, the atmosphere is relaxed and laid back. The menu is an eclectic mix of some Creole dishes and North American-style fare.

Chak Chak
$$$
closed Mon
Beanfield, at Clouds Nest cottages north of Pointe Sable
☎*454-6260*

Spacious and breezy, Chak Chak offers stylish, though casual, dining. Divided into three tiers with a balcony on the water, patrons can choose from a menu of continental and Creole-style meat and seafood, such as the local catch of spiny lobster. The clientele here is mostly made up of a cheery local crowd and tourists.

Vieux Fort and the South

The staff is friendly and attentive.

Juliette's Lodge
$$$$
Beanfield, East Coast Hwy., 500m (1,800ft) south of the airport
☎454-5300
The menu at Juliette's Lodge includes a broad range of items to ensure all guests at the hotel are satisfied. Creole cuisine as well as steak and seafood dishes are offered. The dining area is bright and tables are available on the balcony with a lovely view of the eastern coastline.

Entertainment

Club Exquisite
$20 Sat only
Fri and Sat from 5pm
across from the Skyway Hotel, Vieux Fort
☎454-7131
Club Exquisite is the latest nightspot in Vieux Fort. Fridays, a mix of American and Caribbean music is played on the house sound system. Saturdays, live bands from the Caribbean and the UK are featured. It tends to attract a young crowd.

Reef Café
Anse de Sables, middle of beach
☎454-3418
At one time, the Reef Café had DJs on weekends, but that has stopped, at least temporarily. Call for an update.

Shopping

Saturday Morning Market
Commercial St., by the fish market
For fresh produce and fish, the Saturday morning market is unbeatable. Whatever catch is in season will be available, stacked neatly on a blanket or a table by the road. There are exotic fruits like wax apples, along with grapefruits, pineapple, dasheen, plantain and fresh local spices such as nutmeg, cinnamon and ginger.

Choiseul Arts and Crafts Centre
Mon-Fri 8:30am to 4:30pm, Sat 10am to 2pm
La Fargue, south of Choiseul on the West Coast Hwy.
The Choiseul Arts and Crafts Centre offers a good selection of quality local handicrafts. Everything from traditionally crafted furniture and pottery to wood carvings, baskets, canes, flowerpots and placemats is available. All the items are made with local materials and your purchase helps support the training of local artisans.

The Mid-Atlantic Coast

For many visitors, the Mid-Atlantic Coast ★★ is their first glimpse of St. Lucia as they drive from the airport in Vieux Fort to hotels in the north.

From the highway, the view is perhaps an unsettling contrast to popular images of the Caribbean. Instead of lush tropical forests and white sandy beaches with coconut palms, the landscape looks barren and rocky. A closer look, however, reveals a landscape of uncommon natural beauty. Dramatic vistas have been created by the powerful surf of the Atlantic Ocean, which has carved tiny islands and smooth arches out of the rocky cliffs. At the shoreline, the constant breeze of the northeast tradewinds and open stretches of savannah with exotic cacti and twisted trees, rise gradually up to a mountainous interior of lush forests and fertile valleys.

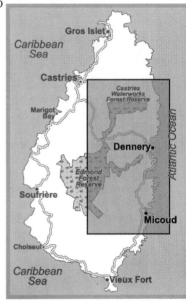

Tourism has a relatively minor presence in the southeast. There are very few hotels or restaurants. It is less travelled, but that can be one of its most alluring charms. In spite of St. Lucia's latest boom in tourism development, this region's economy is still largely dependent on agriculture and fishing. And yet, for nature lovers and outdoor enthusiasts, the mid-Atlantic coast has plenty to offer and it is only a short scenic drive from Castries or Vieux Fort.

On the Eastern Nature Trail, near Dennery, hikers enjoy spectacular vistas of the island's Atlantic shoreline. In summer, Frigate Islands Nature Reserve, in Praslin Bay, is crowded with colourful red-billed tropic birds and scores of magnificent frigate birds soaring gracefully above the water with their impressive wingspans. Inland, it is an altogether different world. At Quilesse Forest Reserve, the Des Cartier Trail leads visitors on an invigorating hike through virgin rain forest while at La Tille, you can explore a riverbed and then swim under a beautiful waterfall. For local history and natural beauty, there are tours of Fond d'Or Estate and Mamiku Gardens.

Finding Your Way Around

This chapter covers the Atlantic side of the island north of Vieux Fort from the quarter of Dennery to Micoud, proceeding in a southerly direction. The East Coast Highway is the only north-south route on this side of the island so it is easy to find your way around. If you are coming from Castries or Soufrière, take the West Coast Highway and head east at the Cul de Sac Junction for Dennery. From Vieux Fort, just follow the East Coast Highway north around Hewanorra International Airport past Savannes Bay and do the tour in reverse.

By Car

Renting a car is a good way to explore the southeast, especially if you are staying in Soufrière or Rodney Bay. There are no car rental agencies based in this region. The nearest outlets are at Hewanorra International Airport in Vieux Fort or downtown Castries. Gas stations are located along the East Coast Highway in Riche Fond, Dennery, Mon Repos and Micoud.

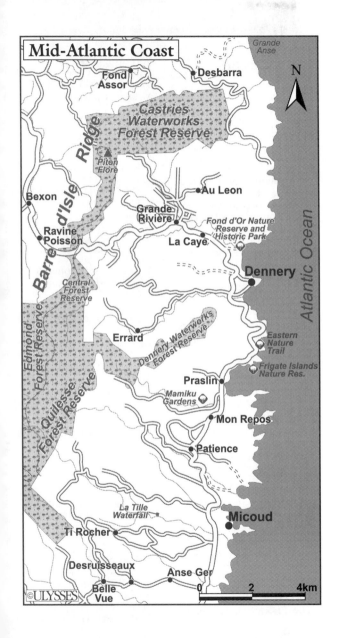

Mid-Atlantic Coast

Grande Anse

Fond Assor

Desbarra

N

Castries Waterworks Forest Reserve

Piton Flore

Bexon

Ravine Poisson

Grande Rivière

Au Leon

Fond d'Or Nature Reserve and Historic Park

La Caye

Dennery

Atlantic Ocean

Central Forest Reserve

Barre d'Isle Ridge

Edmond Forest Reserve

Errard

Dennery Waterworks Forest Reserve

Eastern Nature Trail

Frigate Islands Nature Res.

Quilesse Forest Reserve

Praslin

Mamiku Gardens

Mon Repos

Patience

La Tille Waterfall

Micoud

Ti Rocher

Desruisseaux

Anse Ger

Belle Vue

0   2   4km

©ULYSSES

By Bus

The main bus through this region is route no. 2, which runs regularly along the East Coast Highway between Castries and Vieux Fort. At the main terminal in Castries, Route no. 2c brings you right into Dennery and no. 2e goes into Micoud. The quickest way from Soufrière is to take the bus to Castries and get off at the Cul de Sac junction and wait for an East Coast bus.

By Taxi

The nearest taxi operators are in Vieux Fort or Castries.

Practical Information

For most supplies and services, such as drug prescriptions or foreign exchange, you will have to do as the locals do, and make a trip into Vieux Fort or Castries.

Tourist Information

The closest office of the **St. Lucia Tourist Board** is at Hewanorra International Airport (☎454-6644) in Vieux Fort. Otherwise, staff at your hotel can provide whatever information you need.

Banks

The nearest banks or ATMs are located in Vieux Fort. Some foreign currencies can also be exchanged at your hotel.

Mail

Post offices are open Monday to Friday 8:30am to 4:30pm.

Dennery

Bay St. opposite St. Peter's Church

Micoud

Near the junction of the East Coast Hwy. and the south road into Micoud

Telecommunications

There are public telephones in Dennery and Micoud.

Supermarkets

La Caye

JQ Charles
Mon, Tue, Thu, Sat 9am to 5pm, Wed 9am to 12:30pm, Fri 9am to 7pm
off the East Coast Hwy. north of Dennery, beneath the Greenfield Inn

Police

Dennery

Bay St. opposite St. Peter's Church
☎453-4277

Micoud

along the north road into town by the waterfront
☎454-0708

Exploring

The only tour in this chapter starts on the East Coast Highway as it crosses over the Barre D'Isle Ridge (see Barre D'Isle Ridge Trail p 139) into Grande Rivière, West of Dennery. Near the top of the ridge is a viewing platform that gives you a sweeping perspective of the fertile **Mabouya Valley,** stretching to Fond d'Or Bay and the Atlantic Ocean. To the left is La Sorcière, a mountain surrounded by dense forests that served for many years as an escape route for slaves and brigand rebels. On your right is Mount Beaujolais, which divides the Mabouya Valley from Dennery Waterworks Forest Reserve, a protected watershed area that is not set up for tourists or hikers. The highway quickly descends Barre D'Isle Ridge with several sharp turns into banana and coconut plantations.

The Mabouya Valley has a long agricultural history. The largest area of arable land on this side of the island, it was cleared and divided into estates by French planters at a very early stage of St. Lucia's development. The rich volcanic soil provided tobacco, cotton, sugar cane and now bananas while the Fond d'Or River, which runs the length of the valley, provided irrigation and an energy source to turn the wheels in the mills.

Today, the Mabouya Valley remains an important agricultural area. The even terrain is what makes this one of the few places on the island that is actually suitable for large-scale banana cultivation. Like other island areas heavily dependent on bananas, during the mid-1990s farmers in Mabouya were desperately coping with rapidly falling prices for their crops and conflicts within their own union. When the farmers protested by refusing to harvest their bananas, an already tense situation got worse as other «farmers ignored the ban and went ahead with the harvest. One heated confrontation between farmers and the police near Grande Rivière even resulted in the

St. Lucia's Flag

Fidelity, prosperity, unity and hope.

The vivid sky-blue background of St. Lucia's national flag represents the beautiful Caribbean sky and the waters of the Atlantic Ocean and the Caribbean Sea that surrounds the island. The color blue also stands for fidelity. In the centre of the flag is an isosceles triangle in which three triangles are stacked one upon the other extending from a common base. The lowest and broadest of the three is gold, symbolizing prosperity and the bright Caribbean sun. The other black and white triangles stand for the two major cultures of the island—African and European. The two together signifies unity, with the black being the largest and dominant part. The shape of the triangle refers to the Pitons, St. Lucia's national landmarks. These giant rocks reaching for the sky are considered symbols of the strength and hopes of the Lucian people.

tragic death of a farmer from Riche Fonde. St. Lucia is still recovering from the weakening of its banana industry, but the crisis highlighted the island's vulnerability and the urgent need for economic diversification.

One concrete response by government and the local community is the Mabouya

Valley Development Project. An effort to broaden the economic base of the area beyond agriculture led to the opening of **Fond d'Or Nature Reserve and Historic Park** ★★ *($13; call in advance to arrange tour;* ☎*453-3242)* a short distance south of La Caye on the east side of the highway. It's best to call ahead before you visit the park to find out about cultural events that may be scheduled at the time. Groups can also arrange for Creole meals and folk music demonstrations. Tours of the former sugar plantation combine nature interpretation and local history. Guides point out the medicinal uses of many different herbs and plants found along the way. The tour ends with a hike through a coconut plantation to Fond d'Or Bay and a picturesque beach.

Curving south, the highway passes the western outskirts of **Dennery** ★. A road leading through the centre of town to the water meets the highway at points north and south of town. Due to an early reputation for boat building, using large trees from the nearby forest, Dennery was originally named Anse Canot (*canot* being French for canoe). It was later renamed in hon-

our of Count d'Ennery, governor-general of the French Windward Islands from 1766-70. On a small hill overlooking the waterfront is **St. Peter's Church**, which is appropriately dedicated to fishers. Next to the concrete jetty, there is a rough beach where locals go to cool off. In late June, during the Fishers Festival, the whole community comes out to watch a variety of events, such as the exciting boat races around Denney Island in the middle of the bay.

St. Peter's Church

Farther along, the East Coast Highway crosses Dennery River and then cuts sharply towards the Atlantic coast. At Mandele Point, the **Eastern Nature Trail** ★★★ (see p 216) takes you on a wonderful hike along the Atlantic coast.

Back at the highway, as you begin a gradual descent into Praslin Bay there is a kiosk for **Frigate Islands Nature Reserve** ★★ where you can observe nesting seabirds like the magnificent frigate bird. Across the bay is Martelly Point, a thin finger of land stretching far out into the ocean and once the site of an iron foundry.

The tour continues around the bay through **Praslin**, which was once a busy port town with a church and hospital. Before there were roads on this side of the island and trucks took over as the main source of transport, ships stopped here to pick up produce from the nearby estates and bring it to market in Castries. Praslin is still known as a centre for traditional boat building. If you take the road from the highway down to the shoreline, there is a chance you may see one being built.

As the highway leaves the coast, a sign on the west side shows the way to **Mamiku Gardens ★** *($15; every day 9am to 5pm; ☎455-3729)*. In 1796, Mamiku Estate was the site of a battle between brigand rebels and a British force of mainly black soldiers from Guadeloupe led by a French royalist named Captain de Marchay. The British had taken over the estate, which at the time was owned by Madame de Micoud, to protect the port of Praslin. When the brigands finally attacked, the British force of 70 men was defeated with 15 soldiers killed, and the estate was

burned. A landscape architect has transformed the property into several different tropical gardens of rare flowers, plants and medicinal herbs. Trails lead you through each of the gardens up to the foundations of the 18th-century estate house, where there is a wonderful view of the Frigate Islands and the coconut plantations lining Praslin Bay below. There are also trails through the surrounding forest and a banana plantation. It's a pleasant walk and guides provide insights into the area's history and local uses for many of the plants on the estate.

Farther along, the highway passes through the community of **Mon Repos** before winding inland over the top of a broad ridge past Patience Estate and then sloping down across the Fond River and returning to the coast by the cove of Port Volet. At the next junction, a road leads east into the windswept village of **Micoud**. Like Dennery, the economy of this area depends on fishing and agriculture. Micoud is popular around the island for the large celebrations it holds each year for the Creole festivals of La Rose and La Marguerite (see p 43).

Leaving the spartan coastline behind, our tour turns right at the Micoud junction onto Boiscanoe Road and climbs above the Troumas-sée River into the forested interior. Turn left at the sign for **La Tille Waterfall ★★** (*$10; every day 9am to 4pm; ☎454-0202*). Owner John "Sky" Joseph has created a peaceful nature park in the forest with an interesting trail that explores the river and ravine on the property. You can swim beneath the cascade of a 6m (20ft) water-fall nearby or hike downriver to the ruins of an old mill and a century-old dam. The swim-ming is great and the water is deep enough to enjoy falling off the end of a swinging rope that hangs from a tree. La Tille is a great place for families with small children and a beautiful spot to en-joy a picnic. If you call ahead, a vegetarian meal using ingredients from the garden can be prepared for you. Local handicrafts and fresh jams are also avail-able.

To continue, follow Boiscanoe Road as it winds through the lush green countryside until it eventu-ally crosses a bridge over the Troumassée River, where you turn right onto a rough, narrow road. The further you travel, the more

pot-holed it becomes, a sure sign you are nearing the rain forest. Surrounded by hills and valleys planted with bananas, coconuts and dasheen, the road ends in **Quilesse Forest Reserve**. Here, the **Des Cartier Trail ★★** takes you through the southeastern portion of the island's rain forest (see p 216). Your chances of seeing, or at least hear-ing, the much-cele-brated St. Lucia parrot are fairly good in this area. Among its favourite foods are awali and ti kanot, two creeper plants that gather enough light to survive be-neath the dense forest canopy by attaching themselves to the branches of tall trees.

St. Lucia Parrot

To return to the East Coast Highway, retrace your steps along Boiscanoe Road.

Outdoor Activities

Cruises

Eastern Tours
☎455-3099
Eastern Tours offers boat rides to Praslin Island for

$21 per person. It's a great excursion that gives you a unique view of St. Lucia's Atlantic coastline.

Hiking

One of the best areas to hike on the island is the **Eastern Nature Trail** ★★★ *($32, $82 with a guide; Mon-Fri 9am to 4pm, Sun by appointment; to use the trail with or without a guide call Eastern Tours in advance to have the gate opened at ☎455-3099)*, which is located on the East Coast Highway, south of Dennery. The Eastern Nature Trail offers a very accessible opportunity to experience St. Lucia's rugged Atlantic coastline. Whereas in the northern regions you need a four-wheel-drive vehicle to get across the island, in this case the trailhead is right at the side of the highway. This exhilarating 3hr hike (return) starts near Mandele Point and heads south along the spectacular Atlantic coastline through grassy savannah, tall cacti and short, twisted trees. The rocky shoreline, with its cliffs and interesting rock formations, appears even more dramatic against the rolling surf and the fresh tradewinds blowing in from the northeast. The hike reaches as far south as Praslin Bay on a short peninsula with a brilliant view of the bay and Frigate Islands Nature Reserve (see below). The terrain is not too demanding so it's suitable for families with older children. If you find the distance is too great, there are several exit trails to the highway. You can also pre-arrange a boat ride to the small beach on Praslin Island, where you can enjoy a swim.

At the **Frigate Islands Nature Reserve** ★★ *($13; $53 with a guide; Mon-Fri 9am to 4pm, Sun by appt.; contact Eastern Tours at ☎455-3099)* there is a short trail that connects the southern end of the Eastern Nature Trail (see above) to an observation platform overlooking the Frigate Islands. The reserve's main attraction is its many sea birds, like the magnificent frigate and the red-billed tropic bird, which take over these islands during their migratory season between March and August. Throughout the year, however, you can also see the St. Lucia oriole, tremblers, the ramier pigeon and several reptiles. Boat rides to Praslin Island can be arranged (see p 215).

Situated in Quilesse Forest Reserve, northwest of Micoud, the **Des Cartier Trail** *($25 including guide; Mon-Fri 9am to 4pm; call the Depart-*

ment of Forestry at least 24hrs in advance at ☎450-2231) is a fairly rigorous 4km (2.5mi) trail leading through the natural beauty of a lush rain forest in the heart of the island's southern interior. There are several lookout points with impressive views all the way to Vieux Fort and Micoud. Centuries ago, wider sections of this trail were part of an overland road built by the French military. At the base of Piton St. Esprit (1,919m or 6,300ft), amid gigantic gommier and chatagnier trees, are forest thrushers, tremblers, Adelaide's warblers and beautiful Antillean crested hummingbirds. Mongoose are also commonly found in this region. The Des Cartier Trail also meets up with the Edmond Forest Trail east of Soufrière, which makes it possible to hike cross the island. It is a full-day hike, and highly recommended, but it involves some transportation arrangements to get back to your hotel. However, if you travel lightly and don't mind a bit of walking beyond the trail, you can do the journey without hiring taxis. Before setting out, make sure you understand the route. The Des Cartier Trail is demanding in several sections although steps make it easier and less slippery during the rainy season. Washrooms, drinking water and a sheltered picnic area are available at the trailhead. This is a moderately demanding hike that is a bit too steep in certain sections for young children.

Horseback Riding

Fox Grove Inn
Mon Repos
☎455-3800
The Fox Grove Inn offers half- and full-day rides along the Atlantic coast around Praslin Bay from the Frigate Islands to Martelly Point. Professional riding instruction in English or Western styles is also available in several languages.

Accommodations

Mon Repos

Fox Grove Inn
$169 bkfst incl.
⊗, ≈, ℜ
Mon Repos, off the East Coast Hwy. near Mamiku Estate
☎455-3800
⇄455-3271
www.foxgroveinn.com
On a hill overlooking beautiful Praslin Bay, the Fox Grove Inn offers a relaxing environment away from the busy tourist areas. Each of

the 12 rooms is bright and simply furnished but comfortable, with splendid views of the ocean from a private balcony. Amid the lush surroundings, there is plenty of green space and excellent facilities for those who enjoy horseback riding. The atmosphere is professional but also refreshingly personal and casual.

Desruisseaux

Manje Domi
$156 bkfst incl.
⊗, ℜ
Anse Ger Rd., south of Micoud, off the East Coast Hwy.
☎/⊜455-0729
Situated in the beautiful southern forest region, Manje Domi provides friendly guesthouse accommodation in quiet surroundings. The rooms are comfortable, but a little small, which makes the private patio by the garden indispensable. The Des Cartier Trail is nearby and there are opportunities to explore the immediate area and meet people from the local community.

Restaurants

Mon Repos

Fox Grove Inn
$$$$
off the East Coast Hwy. between Praslin and Mon Repos
☎455-3271
Perched on a slope facing Praslin Bay, Fox Grove Inn is worth a visit for the wonderful scenery. In a friendly setting, the menu features a wide selection of meat and seafood dishes, such as escalopes of kingfish and breast of duck with green pepper sauce.

Desruisseaux

Manje Domi
$$$
non-guests must call in advance to make reservations
Anse Ger Rd. off the East Coast Hwy. near Micoud
☎455-0729
Manje Domi offers tasty Creole cuisine using fresh local vegetables, fruits and seafood from the region. With a reservation, a meal is prepared especially for you to dine outside on the open verandah.

Index

Index

Index

Order Form – Southern Destinations

For a complete list of our guides, please see our web site, below

☐ Acapulco	$14.95 CAN / $9.95 US	☐ Honduras	$24.95 CAN / $17.95 US
☐ Cancún & Riviera Maya	$19.95 CAN / $14.95 US	☐ Huatulco– Puerto Escondido	$17.95 CAN / $12.95 US
☐ Cartagena (Colombia)	$12.95 CAN / $9.95 US	☐ Islands of the Bahamas	$24.95 CAN / $17.95 US
☐ Chile	$27.95 CAN / $17.95 US	☐ Los Cabos and La Paz	$14.95 CAN / $10.95 US
☐ Colombia	$29.95 CAN / $21.95 US	☐ Martinique	$24.95 CAN / $17.95 US
☐ Costa Rica	$27.95 CAN / $19.95 US	☐ Nicaragua	$24.95 CAN / $16.95 US
☐ Cuba	$24.95 CAN / $17.95 US	☐ Panamá	$24.95 CAN / $17.95 US
☐ Dominican Republic	$24.95 CAN / $17.95 US	☐ Peru	$27.95 CAN / $19.95 US
☐ Ecuador and Galápagos Islands	$24.95 CAN / $17.95 US	☐ Puerto Plata– Sosua	$14.95 CAN / $9.95 US
☐ El Salvador	$22.95 CAN / $14.95 US	☐ Puerto Rico	$24.95 CAN / $17.95 US
☐ Guadalajara	$17.95 CAN / $12.95 US	☐ Puerto Vallarta	$14.95 CAN / $9.95 US
☐ Guadeloupe	$24.95 CAN / $17.95 US	☐ St. Lucia	$17.95 CAN / $12.95 US
☐ Guatemala	$24.95 CAN / $17.95 US	☐ St. Martin and St. Barts	$16.95 CAN / $12.95 US

Title	Qty	Price	Total

Name:	Subtotal	
	Shipping	$4.75CAN $3.75US
Address:	Subtotal	
	GST in Canada 7%	
	Total	

Tel: Fax:

E-mail:

Payment: ☐ Cheque ☐ Visa ☐ MasterCard

4176 St. Denis Street,
Montréal, Québec,
H2W 2M5
☎(514) 843-9447
Fax: (514) 843-9448

305 Madison Avenue,
Suite 1166,
New York, NY 10165

Toll-free: 1-877-542-7247
Info@ulysses.ca
www.ulyssesguides.com